Opportunity Meets Motivation
*Lessons From Four Women Who
Built Passion Into Their Lives and Careers*

Marla Brown
Angela K. Durden
Peggy M. Parks
Eleanor Morgan

Opportunity

lessons from four women who

Meets

built passion into their lives and careers

Motivation

BROWN • DURDEN • PARKS • MORGAN

Exterior and interior photos: www.JimChatwinFoto.com
Cover design, interior design and layout: www.AngelaDurden.com

First print run: 1000

ISBN   0-9701356-3-7
ISBN-13 978-0-9701356-3-6

Disclaimer: The information contained in this book is based on the personal experiences of the authors and is not intended as a substitute for advice from those trained in the intricacies of legal and financial issues concerning your situation. Before you set up your own business, please consult an attorney or certified public accountant with details of your situation and check with all governmental entities that will license your business or otherwise have any bearing on where and how you can do business.

Foreword

An organization, regardless of its membership or focus, goes through many stages during its lifetime. One of them comes when members realize that after successfully meeting challenge after challenge, they have amazing stories to tell.

Atlanta Women in Business arrived at that point in 2008, when it was sixteen years old. In this volume, you will find four of our stories, representing just about every phase of a woman's life and career. The authors' individual paths could not be more different, but each came to be a successful business owner in the end.

These are the stories of Angela K. Durden, a stay-at-home mom itching to spread her wings, who spearheaded this project, and Peggy M. Parks, an administrative assistant content to remain in the shadows of the corporate world and whose second book this is. These covers contain the story of hard-charging corporate executive Marla Brown and that of Eleanor Morgan, who always knew what she wanted to be. Their stories illuminate what it means to be not just a business owner, but also a woman business owner.

You will read where they came from, why they became business owners, how they did it, and what you can learn from their experiences. Immerse yourself in their personal stories and then go to the back of this book for practical advice from each of them.

This is a journey of self-discovery, a trek across entrepreneurship, a goodbye to a corporate career. It's real, it's raw, and it's inspirational. They — Angela, Peggy, Marla, and Eleanor — did it. You can, too!

Lya Sorano, Founder & Principal
Atlanta Women in Business • www.atlantawomeninbusiness.com

History of AWIB

Lya Sorano started Atlanta Women in Business in 1992, with the National Association for Female Executives in New York as its model, because there was no organization of its kind in Atlanta — one that welcomed career women as well as business owners and women in the professions, one that identified itself as being inclusive, rather than exclusive. (As long as equality in the business world remains elusive, we cannot afford to exclude even one woman.)

The organization, whose values are authenticity and diversity as well as inclusiveness, provides networking and educational opportunities and is the producer of the first-ever international businesswomen's conference held in Atlanta (Crossing Bridges, 2006). You are invited to be a part of it as we approach our twentieth anniversary, and to add your success story to ours.

Dear Reader

Official statistics about women-owned businesses — updated constantly and found on federal government Web sites — vary widely depending on the criteria of each survey, census, or report. Interpreters of the figures often don't agree on conclusions.

While we will not list any figures here, one thing is clear from every report: Self-employed women are a strong force in the economic health of their households, communities, states, and nation. According to the SBA Office of Advocacy's Small Business Research Summary (Report No. 341), women overwhelmingly use self-employment as a way to balance work and home; time spent in and on their businesses shows their families' needs come first. Men typically base self-employment choices on earning potential and schedule their time accordingly. Neither approach seems right or wrong; they are simply different.

Historically, the number of self-employed men is double that of self-employed women. That brings up an often-asked question: "How can we make these figures equal?" But, as the surveys show, the motivations of each gender do not make for apples-to-apples comparisons, so perhaps the question should be: "How can we encourage more women to seek better balance in their lives and remain economically viable?"

Could it be through self-employment? Quite possibly.

We four are doing that, each differently. We explain those differences in this book. Based on our backgrounds and experiences, we have little in common aside from the fact we are female. Yet each of us, at different stages in our lives, sought some measure of control over our emotional, financial, physical, and spiritual well-being. After searching for how to do it, we each chose self-employment.

There are no one-size-fits-all answers within these pages. How could there be? We are not living one-size-fits-all lives. We four authors sacrificed to get the balance we needed into our lives. In publishing our life/business stories and sharing our different views on the same business issues, we hope to offer encouragement and advice to those who — no matter their situation — seek balance in their lives via self-employment.

Everyone leaves a legacy. What it will be, how it will be built, and whether those left behind are happy to receive it varies by person. We do not claim to have the answers to everything, but we are willing to share what we have learned — warts and all — so that you, the reader, can benefit. We do that by telling what it's like on the front lines and the struggles you will face getting there.

This book — and other venues in which we share the reality and optimism, the pain and happiness, and the costs and rewards of business ownership — is part of our legacy.

We hope you will be encouraged by what you read. We hope you can identify with something in our life stories that will cause you to say, "Hey, that's me!" We hope you overcome the fears — fear of change, fear of an audience, fear of a challenge, and fear of fear itself.

These words about fear are not meant to discourage because there will be fear. We simply wish for you the opportunity to take a path less taken — but only if that path is right for your circumstances. This book is our attempt to shed light on that path.

We hope for the best for you as others hoped for the best for us and, in so doing, gave us the best advice they had at any given time.

Sincerely,

Table of Contents

Table of Contents (continued)

Our Stories

"I continue to live each day
with faith and passion,
always maintaining
an awareness of
new opportunities."

Marla

Life's True Purpose

Marla Brown

www.YouthtopiaMedSpa.com
www.SageMSLA.com

I had finally made it.

I worked for a Fortune 50 company and was in charge of one of the largest districts in the world. I was managing more than four-hundred people, a one-billion-dollar sales plan, and the integration of a newly acquired company. I was living in England and realizing a dream. At only thirty-five years old, I had achieved more financial wealth than anyone in my extended family.

As a young girl, I always envisioned myself as a professional woman wearing a business suit and carrying a briefcase. As such, I was a role model for my daughter and the women who worked for me. I was living this dream for myself and others.

So why did I feel so empty?

It seemed the closer I got to the top of this massive organization, the more disenchanted I became — not only with my job, but also my general purpose in life.

I began management training as a sales representative right out of college. The money was good, with plenty of room for advancement. It was a wonderful company with great people. As a female, I was in the right place at the right time. I quickly excelled, earning promotions that took me across the country and around the world.

I had an insatiable passion for working with people and was inspired by the opportunity to develop front-line employees and solid relationships with customers.

Most importantly, I loved making a difference, especially since I was a minority — a female of prominence in a Fortune 50 company.

Growing up in the corporate culture taught me many things about Corporate America and myself. I learned the value of a strong work ethic to earn my stripes. I learned to be not only more accepting of people, but also more balanced in my approach. Leading instead of merely managing people was important. And issues of profit against revenue growth, as well as personal issues like harassment and inequality of pay and responsibility, were particularly challenging in this environment.

It was a new world full of opportunities to learn and grow. Embracing the culture and challenges, I transformed myself into the person who could succeed in this world. I grew to be more professional, political, and understanding of the dynamics of both the internal and external business going on around me. And I became very good at it.

At the same time, my family and friends could not identify with my new persona. My ten-year-old daughter barely knew me because I was never home. My husband had become a complete stranger. I had a family I couldn't understand or seem to tolerate since they couldn't relate to my world. I was supposed to be at the height of my career and life but had hit rock bottom.

After all those years of working so hard to present a portrait of a successful woman, the person in the mirror was simply tired, confused, overweight, lonely, and depressed. I had lost true purpose in my life.

Then the final shoe dropped. One of the highest ranking women decided I was a star candidate to be groomed for the next level.

All it took was a couple of days shadowing her and my immediate boss for the corporate blinders to be lifted. I had risen to a level within the organization that allowed me a glimpse of decision-making at the very top. Looking closer allowed me to see my future.

While this woman was tough as nails and making a lot of money, she certainly wasn't someone to admire. Like me, she had risen from the front lines. But like her peers, she was a conformist. She chose to turn a blind eye to the true needs of our employees and customers because it was easier and often necessary to agree with the bottom line. The reflection in her eyes showed someone lost, angry, and overworked. Her health was poor, and she was disinterested and uninvolved in my progress and the success of my peers.

Viewed from her perspective, it was easy to understand why she worked the way she did. Within the highly structured corporate environment, the consensus is often more important than individual attitudes and opinions. This form of *groupthink* produces decisions based on assumptions — the way things should be as opposed to how they are. Groupthink creates significant lack of passion for doing the right thing.

It wasn't that I couldn't make a difference within the corporation. Problem was, I would need to conform to be part of the group that was making a difference. But I had already changed too much. I wanted my own identity back — to find my true purpose in both my career and personal life.

Despite fourteen loyal and productive years of service with the company, I left my job. My marriage had ended in divorce. My daughter, a spoiled and unhappy child, needed direction. And I was more lost than ever.

For the first time, I wasn't sure who I was. I'd come so far from where I began that I no longer knew my own identity. A powerful, influential, educated career woman had allowed herself to be defined by a corporation.

Now what? The oldest of four children, and determined to set an example for my siblings, I was also the oldest child of my extended family. There were no female mentors in my family who had the ambition for, much less received, a college degree.

Growing up in a very small town north of Pittsburgh, Pennsylvania, no one was a stranger and everyone liked the consistency of daily family life. At thirteen, I began working at our family bakery business. Edinburg was an old, depressed coal and steel town where most jobs were blue collar, often difficult and backbreaking. My father, a second generation Italian, wasn't convinced his daughter needed a college education — but he wanted to help me succeed.

Working at the bakery taught me that I could continue to be a victim of hourly pay with little room for intellectual creativity or choose to work hard, get an education, and put myself in a position to change things for myself and my family. My mother convinced me that my "free-spirited" attitude would make me very successful at anything I wanted to do in life.

Elected Class President and Treasurer of the Student Council, chosen as Director of the Senior Class Play, School Representative to the regional Young Miss Pageant, "Biggest Daydreamer," and Homecoming Queen, I had a series of accomplishments in high school that catapulted me to the next opportunity. Learning didn't come easy. I had to work harder at my studies than most, but I did get through the testing to get into college.

During my teen years, I collected enough financial assistance for tuition and also worked two jobs during college to help my parents pay the remaining debt. My high school SAT scores caused me to be put on academic probation for the first year of college. But I earned high honors and went on to earn educational scholarships to pay for additional years. During this time, I worked in the public relations office at the university and a local museum and earned my Bachelor's Degree in Communications and Marketing. During my final year of school, I worked an internship with the company that would launch my career.

Marrying my high school sweetheart was the steppingstone into a foreign and benign world. He was educated, a good person, financially secure, and willing to allow me to spread my wings and explore.

Hired out of college as a salesperson by a large multi-national corporation, I found the money better than could be earned in my field of study. Everything seemed to fit into the perfect picture of life. This was the life I had dreamed of and worked so hard for.

I dedicated my heart and soul to learning how to do the job well. While doing so, I also earned a Master's Degree in Organizational Leadership, preparing for a much larger role with the corporation.

My mother was a stay-at-home mom who loved her family and dedicated her life to infusing pride, confidence, and happiness into her children. My dad was an educated entrepreneur, builder, teacher, and musician. He worked four jobs while we were growing up just to provide a comfortable living for his family.

Being married more than forty years, my parents were a clear testimonial to how hard work could pay off. Quite naturally, I wanted to make them proud. After all, they gave me a strong foundation, and I wanted to repay them in kind. Although my parents built the foundation for helping me seek out happiness, I misdirected my ambition toward a lesser goal. I prematurely defined happiness as success with money and power.

It was time to change that.

The genesis for my transformation came from a longtime mentor and friend, Greg Brown.

Greg is a wonderful and complex man possessing a big heart and great character. Respecting my views and loving my passion for growth, he wanted to learn from me as much as I wanted to learn from him. He never tried to steer me in any specific direction. He simply became an effective sounding board, supporter and, eventually, my husband. Greg was the inspiration necessary to reach the next vital plateau in life.

I began researching growing trends, matching them against my own degree of passion in my work. The aging baby boomer generation managed most of the future wealth and was also interested in everything related to anti-aging and improved health. This created a significant opportunity. Of course, I was now of an age that was very interested in looking and feeling as healthy as possible. The medical spa market had personal appeal and would give me a chance to regain passion about life and help women like me feel beautiful from the inside out. At the same time, this provided the opportunity to work closely with employees and customers.

Most importantly, there was more time for myself, my daughter, and my relationship with Greg. Starting a small business was a huge risk and totally out of character for me, but the opportunity invigorated a new sense of purpose.

I loved being in control of my life again.

The change was difficult because it required redefining my concept of success. The corporate culture was so ingrained that I felt nothing different could be good.

Letting go of power, prestige, and monetary rewards was a big change. After having grown up without much money and vowing never to struggle like my parents, here I was back in that same position.

Not only that, my daughter had to live without her father and with a mother she barely knew. My parents also didn't understand the change. I had painted a beautiful portrait of success through my previous place of employment. The change scared them.

Truth be told, it scared me, too.

The Purpose

To overcome that fear, I continually reminded myself of my new purpose, which was driven by three primary components:

- Personal and professional needs
- Financial goals
- My own personal worth

It was important to be more passionate about my work and to have a direct impact on the growth and success of employees and customers. At the same time, it was necessary to define true happiness for my daughter and myself without equating it to financial wealth. I needed to have a purpose all my own to work toward.

Emotional stability is reached when the scales of work and home are in balance. At the height of my career, my scales were grossly tilted toward work. I had allowed my concept of success to be dictated by the goals of a multi-national corporation that primarily needed to impress shareholders.

My prestige in Corporate America was based on producing revenue growth. I misdirected my personal need for having a powerful relationship with my God, spouse, and child. My prestige in my home, church, and community was nonexistent.

Trying to live two lives — defining myself one way at home and another at work — was difficult. Each day, the pressure at work caused me to live life as it was defined by the corporation. That pressure was killing me.

I needed to get back to knowing myself to understand how to make the changes. What was most important to me? What attributes did I want to define me? What did I want out of life?

With the same focus I had shown in my teens toward becoming a successful businesswoman, I set out to find the answers.

My professional needs and goals needed to support my personal life while making use of all my business knowledge, training, and varied interests. Opening my own business gave me an opportunity to explore.

My personal interests had been ignored for quite some time. For example, I love art and any activity related to artistic development. I'm also a deeply religious person, despite having drifted away from church. I combined the two and became a liturgical decorator for my church. Tapping into the creative side enabled me to become the ultimate driver of my success. In this area, I could be as creative as possible without fear of being criticized for going outside the groupthink mentality. The flexibility of my new schedule allowed me to explore and expand in these areas. Of course, the lack of corporate stress complemented this goal.

Financial goals needed to be incorporated into my plan to accomplish more balance in life. Making a living from my own small business was important, not running a multi-million-dollar business. Balance necessitated a six-figure salary sacrifice.

Owning my own business was a new way of life. My mother always said, "You need money to make money." I found that to be absolutely true with this new life, working to make it succeed. Like Mom said, money was important in determining how quickly I could grow the medical spa business.

But now money wasn't the engine driving me. It was simply a tool to accomplish something better.

It was a huge risk investing fourteen years of savings into the medical spa. Even then I underestimated the capital necessary to sustain this type of business. Determining how much capital to invest at startup was based on the appeal to an affluent market.

Medical requirements also pushed hard against financial boundaries, requiring additional licensing and insurance as well as special equipment and a professional staff fully versed in the proper use of it. My facilities had to meet a more stringent building code than other types of businesses.

Outside income is often important during the initial building of a business. My ability to secure initial loans and funding was handicapped without the security of having a full-time job. Greg's financial guarantee afforded me this privilege. The advantage of no longer being employed, though, was that there was no financial way out. This business had to succeed or I would lose everything.

The cushion of a day job during the startup might have caused me to give up more easily.

Running my own district in Corporate America allowed me to believe I could do anything. I led and managed very large teams with lofty and far-reaching goals. It would be a snap to effectively manage a small group of employees. Small business does not run like big business, though, as I would soon find out.

In Corporate, teams readily give advice and make recommendations. Colleagues help strategize and share ideas. In the small business environment, it made sense to hire a consulting firm from California comprised of experienced medical and spa professionals. They advised on legal issues and made recommendations on the market, site, personnel, marketing, products, and services.

Entering a medical field with no medical experience, I had to rely on my strong management, marketing, and sales experience. I also had experience with customer service, advertising, and human resource issues. Yet how would these strengths bring value to the business? In other words, how would these help this business be profitable? The answers to these questions identified my true personal worth to the company.

My background enabled me to make informed decisions about how to apply the consultant's recommendations to my specific market needs. Not having much experience or interest in accounting and financial planning, or medical or legal issues, I required additional staffing help.

I thought I was intimately acquainted with my customer and assumed she had the same needs I did. Had I not learned quickly how very wrong I was, the broad and general assumptions made would have sabotaged my success in this complex market. Because the market was diluted with competitors, the consumers' ideas of their needs were varied and their understanding of my business was not clear.

It was important to know my employees' jobs inside and out, especially when they involved new and necessary service options and procedures. I wrote service protocols and expectations. Wearing both owner and management hats, I also had to understand all equipment and product capabilities and comparisons within the industry. My personal value to the company would continue to grow and evolve.

To help focus on where to start, I went back to basics. What was my business and how could I be the ultimate professional with my customers? The answer: skin care. I became well-versed in it and took control of my own skin care program. I began experimenting with all our services and product options. Using and testing each product and service, I quickly identified what wasn't working and moved them out of our lineup. I was free to be passionate about and could wholeheartedly recommend each of the remaining products and services.

I became a walking testimonial. If I looked great, so would our customers. My value to the business included attracting clients. New clients meant my employees would have a job and I would make a profit.

The Foundation

Being in Corporate so long strengthened my appreciation for teams and the value of different viewpoints. The medical spa business was a new industry, and the learning curve was huge and had to be mastered quickly. I couldn't do it alone. Therefore, the consulting firm served as a strong early support network and solid foundation.

The makeup of competitors became more obvious at seminars and meetings with other medical spa owners. In an attempt to escape the medical insurance wars, many doctors were entering this field. They had an intimidating twofold advantage. They could perform simple esthetic services, such as injecting Botox®, at their spas. They could also perform high-end services such as plastic surgery, which would offset some startup and employee costs.

The competition needed someone to market for them. More importantly, they needed to be able to determine whether the person they hired was effective at sales and marketing. This is very difficult when you have no experience with it. It also takes a lot of time. Therefore, the advantage I had over competitors was business knowledge and experience. Effectively planning and executing marketable strategies, I could change my plans on the fly. I could more quickly respond to a change in customers' needs or the financial climate affecting customer spending.

Hiring a Medical Director and paying her a monthly fee to oversee our practice provided financial flexibility while enabling me to retain all the rights and responsibilities for my own business. Hiring a variety of duplicate staff members and specialties allowed flexibility with scheduling and pay.

Ours needed to be a diverse business with attractive service options that would be convenient for customers. The staff had to be able to respond effectively to these needs. This would make us different enough from a doctor's office that customers would feel comfortable and welcomed in our environment, but similar enough that we would still convey the same medical standards, cleanliness, and professionalism expected from a high quality medical practice.

Research in this industry unveiled the worldwide potential. It took me some time to comprehend that it didn't necessarily apply to my market.

Alpharetta, Georgia, was one of the wealthiest cities in the country and one of the most competitive markets for medical spas. Demographics and income levels defined the opportunity. There were five medical spas within a five mile radius. There were also about twenty renowned plastic surgeons in a ten mile radius, half of which were opening medical spas inside their existing practices.

Competition would also come from day spas, facilities that didn't offer nearly as many services. Potential customers did not understand the differences between and the benefits of a medical spa versus a day spa. Consumer education became a major part of my marketing strategy.

Understanding the characteristics of the people I needed walking through my doors helped me design the competitive strategy. In addition, the business needed to reflect an impression of who I was as the owner and what our business was about. This information would be used to build a service menu, brand concept, and marketing campaign, and to help design the interior and architectural design of the spa. The brand name and logo would marry the company's vision, values, and philosophies with the clients' interests. To accomplish this took time and effort to focus on fonts, colors, and symbols to reflect an appropriate image.

The service menu includes a variety of services and options in a non-intimidating environment. The products and equipment vendors need to have the same high standards expected of the staff. Product brands reflect my brand, so it was important to choose the right ones. The interior design of the spa needs to visually communicate our concept and give a positive sensory experience. Color schemes and the progressive flow of the entryway to the rooms set the correct tone. Our Web site, brochures, and all advertising follow suit.

Once we had a brand name, we needed brand awareness. I employed a comprehensive marketing campaign that included radio, print, trade shows, editorials, sponsorships, e-marketing, postcards, and word-of-mouth throughout the Atlanta market. We used various methods to introduce our brand and gain awareness. Coining the phrase "Because Everyone Deserves to Feel Beautiful," we wanted our consumer to understand our goals. This market strategy continued into our second year, when we fine tuned our reach to just the Alpharetta market.

Each day presented learning opportunities about the market and target customer. There were continuous adjustments to the strategy and choreographing of my initiatives. With more knowledge came reassurance that the consultant's value was diminishing. They could educate only on the generalities of the medical spa market. I needed to customize my business to a unique community of buyers. I took on this goal with a fiery passion and continued the necessary research to distinguish Youthtopia from other spas. Sorting through employee and customer issues allowed us to quickly improve methods and processes. Continually assessing the competition allowed us to adjust campaigns to more effectively respond to the needs of our customer. This involved acute attention to detail. As the owner, I needed to be talking to and interacting with customers and employees daily.

My eagerness and fear of failure affected day-to-day decision-making more than I thought it would. Now that it was my money going out the door, I needed to make even more precise decisions about spending it. This needed to be balanced against the company's need for new and exciting marketing strategies and ideas. My immediate decisions would affect every direction of my company. It was a new challenge and opportunity.

It didn't take long to understand why ninety percent of all businesses fail in their first year. My consultants assured me profitability after six months — a prediction as shortsighted as it was unrealistic. Not only did I need to brace myself for three years of potential losses before I saw growth, the economic recession would make my success very unpredictable.

A support network was important to progress. Greg stepped in and became more involved in day-to-day decisions. Needing a sounding board — other business minds with which to share ideas — I befriended several successful businesswomen in the community, listening and learning from their experiences. Some true friends and mentors from my previous place of employment gave me feedback and advice. Respecting their views and opinions, I effectively relied on their support and belief in my ability to grow the new company. Although it was my own business, I was reconfirming the belief that success is never something you truly accomplish alone.

At the same time, I became involved in several women's networking groups whose members were either in the process of starting or had already started businesses. It was inspirational to be around so much energy and passion. I also partnered with other local small businesses to find synergistic ways we could attract our target customer.

As I took a more personal interest in my clients, I found that many brought a unique perspective and had an interest in my growth. In short order, the synergy multiplied and the network began to support me. Prior to this, I waited for business to take off without fully understanding that I needed to be the catalyst for growth.

Growing up within the embrace of Corporate America, there was always a team eager to help identify any potential warning signals. Mistakes there weren't as costly to me compared to what I was going through as a business owner. This was the biggest management role of my life. Whatever mistakes there were to be made and whatever penalties there were to be borne were mine alone.

The responsibilities and challenges were exciting, but the fear of failure was a constant dark cloud. I continually reminded myself of my new purpose in life. Staying focused on my daughter, now blossoming under the growing attention of her mother, made the financial sacrifices worthwhile. I wouldn't trade that for any position of glory or pot of gold in the world.

The Plan

The advice of consultants helped me create an elaborate business plan, but elaborate did not mean accurate. Overly excited about the new business and its growth potential, I relied on their assurances much more than I should have. The costs of building my own brand and business required more evaluation of vendors, location, and pricing than the plan could anticipate.

The initial business plan included health benefits for employees, a large staff, a marketing director, a big marketing budget, beautiful furniture and decorations, full product inventories, and extra money for detail items such as fresh flowers, oranges and apples in the lobby, complimentary Elixir tonics and teas, a complimentary paraffin wax dip for the client's hands while she received a facial, and chocolates on every treatment bed embossed with the Youthtopia logo.

Beautiful robes and lab coats were embroidered for our clients and staff. Our company bags and gift certificates conveyed the same elaborate theme. Extra money was allocated for monthly events at the spa with themes like "Ladies Night Out" and "Lunch and Learn." Finally, my plan included a percentage of profit for the consultant.

There was an existing site in Alpharetta where a day spa had gone out of business. Its design saved money on the build-out. High startup costs would dramatically impact growth, so this location seemed like a smart move. It was twenty-five-hundred square feet and perfectly located on a main road inside the medical corridor of Alpharetta.

We started small and added service options as we generated revenue. Our options needed to be comprehensive and unique. The client needed to see advantages in coming to a medical spa rather than a dermatologist's or plastic surgeon's office. Combining laser services with injectables, we developed service offerings like the "liquid face lift." A unique company in California had a patented way of extracting stem cells from adult adipose tissue. I could help them launch what we were calling "the new age insurance policy" for healthy adults. We also experimented with personal training and did some work with a dietician and a weight management physician. The pursuit for creative options was endless. Finding the right mix for the client that would keep us competitive and cutting edge was my ultimate goal.

Leasing space and equipment rather than purchasing freed up more cash to invest in products and employees. Bank lenders and Small Business Administration loans eased the stress on cash reserves. This was vital and enabled us to continue investing when, because of the recession, banks froze all small business loans.

A doctor in the market did not have the same success. He opened a spa quite close to me with an oversized, highly advanced facility. His high-rent location in a new shopping district required a full build-out and a very large and expensive staff. Adding to his overhead, he purchased all of the up-to-date equipment and products. He was out of business in six months. This trend continued with competitors dropping around me as we fought to maintain market leadership at the lowest possible cost.

It would have been easy to make the same mistake as that doctor. As a technician (as opposed to an entrepreneur), he was convinced of his quick success yet failed to see potential obstacles. *(Publisher's Note: See Chapter 5's first question for an explanation of technician versus entrepreneur.)*

Research proves that most technician-based businesses fail because the technician is never an effective manager. People who are very good at one skill try to open a business performing that particular skill but can never effectively lead a group or form a strategy. Fortunately I was trained at both, having worked my way up from a salesperson to upper management, and had much experience alternating these roles.

Overwhelmed by my roles, I hired a manager to handle marketing and communications. She needed to be someone who reflected our brand, who could attract potential customers by her appearance, knowledge, and passion for our industry, and who could find pockets of clients and business opportunities in the community. But it was impossible to find someone affordable who could both do the job and meet high expectations.

After hiring and firing three people and losing money doing it, I realized the need to also take on this role. Marketing and communications were my strengths. The consulting firm advised that it would be best for me not to take this additional responsibility as it would cause me to deviate from my strategy and management responsibilities. But I decided to capitalize on my strengths and hire people in areas where I was not as strong.

Learning more about the business unveiled opportunities to save money. For instance, there were clients who would trade work like accounting, Web design, window cleaning, advertising, and printing for spa services. Employees also took on more work and responsibility, including cleaning, prospecting for new customers, working the front desk, updating reports, maintaining our database, and evaluating vendors.

Vendors and alliances were filtered based upon their support of the business. Personal services were chosen from people who supported the business in some way. This allowed flexibility to create trade accounts and synergistic relationships for various products and services.

Vendors were selected based on the type of investment they made in my advertising. For instance, my Allergan® rep created and paid for the mailing of postcards to customers. She and other vendors sponsored customer appreciation events. These helped me create a powerful dynamic throughout my customer base. Within two years, many vendors afforded us premier status as one of their top accounts, allowing more flexibility in purchasing options; these discounts could be passed on to customers.

The staff began to think like me in the areas of marketing and sales. Skin care specialists primarily like to help other people feel better about themselves, but they aren't averse to making money. We developed a sales and commission plan that helped them accomplish both.

Grass-roots marketing was powerful. I planted the seeds of skin care and anti-aging techniques at the gym, at my daughter's school, and in the neighborhood with influential women who loved to promote the newest and hottest thing on the market. This gave them something beneficial to pass along to their friends.

I also began an advice column in a local community magazine.

The business was positioned as the "Ritz-Carlton" of our industry, offering a superior experience at a higher price. This was a point of differentiation from the area's other medical spas, which relied on low price and poor service. To set my spa apart, I had to build a staff that would not only treat the customer right but could also effectively work together.

It is no exaggeration to say that the solidarity of a staff is the single most effective tool against the competition. Building this solidarity took time, effort, and turnover. In Corporate America, employees were more career-oriented. Hard work could advance both their career and financial wealth, and the company could count on them being there for a long time because they had these benefits. This is not necessarily true in a small business; the employees may not have the same stability and rewards.

Our mission statement touts that we will have a world class spa and staff. While we ultimately accomplished this, it took two years of consistent turnover and alterations to both pay and commission structures and evaluation techniques. Today, this is our best-known advantage. The amount of time and attention employee issues demanded directly affected how much time could be spent on planning. I took an active role in managing and setting staff expectations. This would set the tone for everything else.

The public was already apprehensive about new medical spas showing up in their community. Until we had consistency within our spa, potential clients would not associate our brand with high quality service and expectations.

To help my employees understand what we were about, the mission statement was employed throughout our culture at the spa. It is displayed in the lobby and on the back of our business cards. We also show it prominently on our Web site, enabling potential clients to make educated decisions about our services. It establishes a big commitment behind the brand and is our blueprint of success for the employees. It reads as follows:

Youthtopia Med Spa will provide safe and effective services administered by a professional, qualified and caring staff with the intent of helping each of our clients feel beautiful and stay healthy. We will achieve this by first employing and training a world class team. In addition, we will provide cutting edge technology and a regimen of the highest quality of products, supplement the education of our employees and community, participate in philanthropic pursuits that benefit our clients' health and ultimately create a profitable business capable of reinvestment. We will administer our services in a clean and healthy environment with a unique, customized and empathetic customer service approach. We will be admired for our attention to detail and focus on our customers' needs.

This is a written acknowledgment of the type of service customers should receive at Youthtopia. As the owner, my goal is to ensure this realization and experience with clients. Both are accomplished through effective communication with the staff.

That same message and the value it promotes is communicated when we participate in local events, thereby building good community relations. We live out our mission by sponsoring several philanthropic community events — promoting things like breast cancer awareness and supporting battered and abused women and disadvantaged children. The bottom line? Our business has been named "The Best Spa in Alpharetta" by the readers of *Around Town* magazine for three consecutive years, "Most Admired" by users of CitySearch, and "The Best of Alpharetta" by the United States Commerce Association.

I never stop searching for new options, alternatives, and positive outcomes. I continue to insist on high quality and make no compromises for cheaper alternatives. I am the heartbeat of my business. I determine the rate of growth based upon my time investment.

The Expectations

As an experienced and educated businesswoman, I was susceptible to the pitfalls of opening a small business. Rushing right out of the corporate world into a small business, I did not completely understand the major differences between the two or the time and money necessary to learn a new industry. In Corporate, positive and negative feedback is constant, providing a gauge for future moves. Ownership, however, was new territory with no clear guide or compass.

After nine months, the working capital — or money left after paying expenses — was just about gone. Early on, it was easy to try a variety of marketing campaigns, test product lines, and invest in training without much thought or concern about the costs or fear of failure. As we progressed, I didn't see the immediate return on these investments, and my war chest was not being replenished. Cutbacks were necessary to continue to operate.

How could the business continue to thrive in a declining economy? I didn't want to become one of the sad statistics that were occurring around me, even in this most affluent of cities. I evaluated the spa's hours, each marketing campaign's effectiveness, inventory turns; in fact, all business costs. Actual results against both my business and sales plans were monitored and altered if necessary. Employees were put on performance-improvement plans, and vendors and products were reevaluated.

We began closing on Mondays. We also shortened hours, consolidated appointments, worked several employees as part-time instead of full-time, eliminated benefits and my personal pay, and bartered with vendors and advertisers instead of paying cash. I also looked at new options for renting equipment instead of leasing to own. These changes kept my business image on the cutting edge without long term financial constraints.

My only gauges were my gut and my conscience, and I had to set goals and assess my progress. I went from a very stable financial future to a very unpredictable and uncomfortable one.

The penalties for making the wrong decisions were no longer just a line item on a monthly report. Causing unnecessary frustration, I set my business goals too high. Due to my initial funding, a profit was necessary in the first year. The stress of not producing one caused me to consider selling the business at a loss or prematurely declaring bankruptcy.

But when the business did not grow as expected, I didn't hide my head in the sand pretending everything was fine. The needs of the business changed because of the economy, location dynamics, the needs of my customers, technology, and local and governmental regulations. Success depended on our ability to adjust plans and expectations on a regular basis. Doing so required not only more money, but also more energy, new ideas, and the ability to swallow my personal pride.

I also set high goals for my staff. I wanted a world class staff from day one, yet was unprepared and impatient with how long it would take to find and train the right people.

Finally, I set my personal goals too high. Quite naturally, I wanted to prove something to myself. This was a new world in which I needed to learn, grow, and succeed to convince myself that I had made the right decision to leave the corporate world.

The skill set of an entrepreneur is unique — one best learned with special doses of patience and faith. My husband often reminded me that I provided myself the most expensive and rewarding MBA possible — one that came with actual experience. This skill set is something you can't learn in the corporate world or the classroom.

In small business, it is important to be flexible and not take everything to heart; this despite the investment of time and money, commitment, and the desire for everything to be positive.

One business constant is the need to always look for growth opportunities. Business and opportunity don't just happen. And never underestimate the power of any relationship or interaction with a customer or colleague. I am a big believer that everything in our lives has a purpose.

We simply need to have the willingness to see and the motivation to work toward the opportunity being presented to us.

The saying "never let them see you sweat" applies equally to owners of both large and small businesses. Employees and customers should never sense the owner's financial insecurities. As far as my customers are concerned, our business is world class, proactive, and growing, despite what is going on in the economy around us. For example, when times got really tough, we bartered for carpet and paint in the offices. We also explored partnerships with local physicians to offer different and exciting services at the spa. Our actions expressed a positive image of growth even when profits were low.

Owning my own business has taught me to have more faith in my decisions. The downside of coming from Corporate America was the need to constantly question myself. For every major decision, feedback was necessary from peers. Every decision was evaluated and reevaluated by my manager. Isolated decisions were seldom made because they had repercussions among other departments or divisions.

It is important to be perceptive enough to evaluate decisions after taking action, identifying if and when change is necessary. Making mistakes is inevitable; the key is knowing how to properly respond. The blending of staff and services, characteristics of the market, and the image we want creates a dynamic experience different from the competition. This requires constant attention.

The Rewards

A small business owner can easily give up when the going gets tough and there is no clear indication which direction is correct. Learning from trial and error can produce a stronger businessperson. You may as well expect to lose some hard-earned money. Still, trial and error can produce benefits. I am a better businessperson, mom, wife, and daughter than I ever could have been had I not made the change to be in business for myself.

For this reason, I am wealthier than ever. Of course, I define my fortune differently since my move from Corporate America.

Although everyone does not take the same path or learn the same way, finding balance and happiness in life is important. I did it by having true purpose interwoven throughout my personal and professional goals and being open to the opportunity to change.

One of those additional opportunities came when I realized I was providing a great spa experience in a down market. With this asset, I set up my own consulting business to assist new business owners desiring to open medical spas (www.SageMSLA.com).

With experience, it is important to trust initial insight and have faith in the outcome. I used to look back with regret on the decision I made to sell my old company's stock to support the new business. However, had I not sold when I did, the stock would have been worth half of its value after the market crash, and I would not have a tangible business asset.

Although owning my own business required creativity and exploration into unknown areas, the large risk was in proportion to the reward. Hard work, indeed, does pay off. It's a great feeling for me to have developed a strong, educated, and cohesive team. It's very rewarding to know that I am a positive contributor to the economic health of my community and family.

Today the Youthtopia brand is one the community associates with high quality, integrity, and trust — a brand that symbolizes not only a business but also a commitment to a worthy cause. This is a great accomplishment for any business owner.

It is important that I continue to stay focused on my personal goals to be more successful with my professional goals. For me, this means more time with my family and doing the activities I love. I now have clear direction and purpose in life. I continue to live each day with faith and passion, always maintaining an awareness of new opportunities.

At the same time, I have more personal satisfaction because I am working for a greater purpose. All of which is the greatest gift I can give to my daughter, my family, my community, my God, and ultimately myself.

Marla Brown

Youthtopia Med Spa is a world class skin rejuvenation and total body wellness spa. The inviting and tranquil environment, coupled with the latest in anti-aging medical procedures, makes it the perfect oasis to begin your personalized beauty plan.

Youthtopia Med Spa• (770) 772-4806

3665 Old Milton Parkway • Suite 30 • Alpharetta, Georgia 30005

marla@youthtopiamedspa.com • www.YouthtopiaMedSpa.com

Sage MSLA • (770) 772-7242

3665 Old Milton Parkway • Suite 40 • Alpharetta, Georgia 30005

marla@sagemsla.com • www.SageMSLA.com

Atlanta Women in Business (www.atlantawomeninbusiness.com)

National Association of Women Business Owners (www.nawbo.org)

e-Women Business Network • Spas Worldwide

Medical Spa MD • Botox Beauties in Alpharetta

"I felt initially that I wasn't worthy.
I was having so much fun, how could I charge people for my services?"

Peggy

Voilà!

Peggy M. Parks
AICI CIP

www.TheParksImageGroup.com
http://PeggyParks.Wordpress.com

There were 103 of them.

I know, because I counted as they entered the room. One-hundred-and-three accomplished businesswomen, eager to learn what I, Peggy Parks, could teach them about the impact of a professional image. And the most remarkable thing was that I felt perfectly at ease, in control, and more powerful than I had ever been.

What a contrast with just three years earlier, when the idea of making a presentation to three department heads in my company would cause my palms to sweat and my voice to quiver, and more often than not turn my stomach into a burning cauldron.

The changes started long before I was even aware of my circumstances and the forces that would influence my life for decades to come. What would have been a normal life in an East Coast suburb came to an abrupt end when I was only two and my father died.

My American father met my French mother after World War II in France. He immediately fell in love and promised to come back for her, which he did. They married in Marseille, where she lived with her parents, and he began working for the American government in Paris and later in Germany. When his contract was up, he decided he and his wife should move to New Jersey, his home state, and that's where I was born.

Unfortunately, when I was two, my father died in an accident, leaving my mother alone in a foreign country with a small child.

She decided to go back to France, seeking solace with her mother, a natural thing to do. My grandmother was French and worked in the haute couture industry. My life was no longer normal to an impressionable little American girl. I discovered, albeit subconsciously, that there is such a thing as "style." My grandmother's early imprint allowed me to grow up with a sense of balance and proportion and a recognition of "fit" in one's attire.

Soon after our move to France, my mother met a Frenchman who had emigrated to French Guiana, on the northern coast of South America, and from there to Venezuela, where he had detected the same kinds of opportunities the United States offered in the first half of the twentieth century. But his language was French, not English, and this had determined his decision and his destination.

My mother and future stepfather had a long-distance relationship over several years, and that's when I started traveling from one continent to another and had to go to new schools and learn a new language every year. Looking back, I feel it was a great experience to be able to assimilate into different cultures, make new friends, and live in places where people spoke different languages — French in France, English in the U.S., and Spanish in Venezuela.

At the same time, I was very shy and timid. When I lived in France with my grandmother, my extended family always wanted me to "say something in English" to show my cousins how smart I was, but I would just clam up and feel embarrassed. I didn't like being the center of attention and felt like the oddball instead of the smart little girl who spoke two or three languages. When my mother and stepfather married, I moved to Venezuela with them at the age of nine, my third country of residence before I even reached adolescence.

Life in Caracas was as normal as one might imagine — certainly I did not know any other — but the early imprint of my mother as dependent on male support was reinforced during my adolescent years. Although I never felt deprived of anything, it was always made clear that Papa (her husband, my stepfather) worked very hard, and we must not do anything extravagant or spend money on things we did not need; we lived frugally, but happily.

Being scared, feeling insecure, and totally lacking in self-confidence was part of my growing-up experience. I remember once being chided by my mother for not saying hello to a little girl with whom I was going to school. We were walking down the street and ran into the little girl and her mother. My mom greeted the other mother while I was hiding behind my mother's skirt. I was afraid to say hello. My mom was indirectly teaching me good manners, but I didn't get it. I was scared.

I went to a British school in Caracas and at first I refused to learn how to speak Spanish. I felt I didn't need to because I spoke English at school (not very well) and French at home. If I needed to speak to anyone in a store or on the street, my mom was there to speak for me.

The best part of growing up in Venezuela was the arrival of my brother Francis, when I was thirteen; I immediately adored him. We formed a bond that gets stronger every year and I only wish we did not live continents apart.

Just as my childhood years had been spent in three countries, so it was with my education. First the British school and then the Colegio Francia in Venezuela, then on to Martinique, where I studied philosophy and languages and obtained my Baccalaureate, and finally, upon my stepfather's insistence, the United States, for college and English.

When I arrived in the U.S., my English was deplorable and my accent was very thick and very French. I attended business school in St. Petersburg, Florida, and no one understood what I was saying. I had to repeat everything two or three times and often became embarrassed, feeling inferior to the other kids. Some of the people I hung around with made me feel like I was from somewhere in space. Many people had never heard of Venezuela and thought I was Italian (as in Venice). I once had a blind date with a guy who, when he picked me up, said, "So, I hear you're from Czechoslovakia." Was my English that bad or were these people unworldly? I became more and more bashful and vowed to learn to speak English the American way. I did so well that today I no longer have a French accent, and I regret that. My mother has a beautiful French accent when she speaks English, and people love to listen to her.

I thought at one time that I might want to be a psychologist and open a practice, but the early imprint of my stepfather the businessman got in the way; I was out of college and had to find a job. That's the way my world appeared to me and it was a pattern I not only thought I had to follow, but was also sketched out by Papa.

"Business," he explained, "is where the money is, not in psychology." He knew. Having arrived alone in South America from France, he had become a self-made man, comfortable in the business world and constantly teaching us to save, save, save.

While I was still in school, someone mentioned I should model because I was tall. It was an exciting proposition, but I was scared to death and knew Papa would have said that modeling was too frivolous and I had to stick to business. There is a delicious irony in the fact that the photographer who assisted us with this book saw my potential as a model, put a portfolio together, and is introducing me to talent agencies. For one thing, I am no longer scared. But it took a long time to get there.

I entered the business world totally lacking in self-confidence. Women were, in a few places, beginning to assert themselves, but for the most part we were receptionists, secretaries, and PBX operators. I stuck the "admin" label on myself and kept it there for two decades. I know my lack of self-esteem kept me from wanting to get out of my comfort zone, but I also realize I learned a great deal from my experiences, both in running a business and in human behavior. But "running a business" is something that never occurred to me until it was the only choice left, and that was many years in the future.

My first decade in the business world was spent in the Tampa Bay area in Florida, working for a financial planner (another frugal, hardworking, self-made man who was driven and expected his employees to be; it was a

24/7 job). I was happy in my comfortable rut, but my husband was transferred to Atlanta, so we moved to a city I thought was bigger than Tampa (true) and more international (not necessarily true), giving someone who spoke three languages an advantage.

Even though the Atlanta employment market required Japanese and German as international languages and mine were French and Spanish, I landed a job as an administrative assistant at Sea-Land Service, where I spent the next eleven years. Every time a promotion opportunity came along, I was petrified that I would get the job and have to travel or, even worse, speak to a group.

I sometimes think of those years as my lost decade. But a connection was being made inside me, subconsciously, with my earlier life — living with my haute couture grandmother in France and my stunningly beautiful and stylishly dressed mother in Venezuela — and I now know my Sea-Land career was a link in the work experiences that got me to where I am today. My co-workers commented on how well I dressed and how professional I looked. They asked what I was doing there and said I should be in fashion instead of shipping. To me, blinders very much in place and self-esteem still frozen at below zero, "fashion" meant retail in a department store. I might be an admin, but I did not want to be a shop girl, so I shrugged it off.

A big change in my life occurred when Sea-Land underwent a corporate takeover. My boss, the Director of Sales, left to take a position at Hitachi and told me he would find me a job there as well. Good to his word, a few months later, no longer an admin, I filled an HR slot at Hitachi as liaison between headquarters and five sales offices, culminating in the position of the division's HR Manager. I still did not consciously know it, but my self-esteem was beginning to rise, at last.

Not my comfort level, though!

Twice a year, the Vice President of Sales and I drove to Greenville, South Carolina, to present our budgets to the corporation's American and Japanese executives. When it was my turn to speak, I would perspire profusely, get red blotches on my neck, breathe heavily, and hear my voice shoot up an octave or two. It was petrifying.

One fine winter's day it all came to an end. Our division of Hitachi was not doing well, the sales offices were closing, and I was out of a job, the best job I'd ever had, a job I had loved for four years. "Now what?" I wondered. "Who is going to hire me now, at my age, a philosophy major bound by fear, unwilling to learn anything that is out of my comfort zone in case I fail or appear stupid?"

And that is how, at the age of fifty, I left Corporate America and became a business owner.

Four things were of immediate benefit: I took time to make an inventory of my skills, experiences, and interests; I had a great experience with the outplacement firm to which Hitachi sent me; I had a friend who had just quit her job and excitedly started a business ("She did it; wonder if I can too?"); and I had — still have — a wonderfully supportive husband, who one day whispered two words: "image consultant."

Of course!

Throughout my corporate life people had come into my office to check out what I was wearing. Men came in to ask if their ties looked right; women asked if I would go shopping with them. Once I had an assistant who asked me to help her find a wedding dress. I often was told I should be "in fashion," but it had not made an impression.

Now I knew and, with great determination, started to take the necessary steps: school (London Image Institute), professional association (Association of Image Consultants International), learning how to speak (Toastmasters), business name, legal structure for my business, business license, Web site, business cards — and waited for the phone to ring.

It didn't.

All my friends congratulated me on becoming a business owner, admired my logo, and told me how spectacularly successful I was going to be. So why weren't people calling?

Lesson number one: To make a business work, the owner has to be willing to work long hours, go out and meet new people constantly, and let them know about the business.

Lesson number two followed quickly: I did not charge enough. I felt initially that I wasn't worthy. I was having so much fun, how could I charge people for my services? The owner of the London Image Institute corrected my thinking; I raised my fees (although not as high as she recommended).

The third lesson is one we all face sooner or later — truly, the sooner the better: You've got to believe you can do it, or it's not going to happen! I was scared and had never wanted to stretch myself, but once I started to believe I could actually do this thing — run a business and make it a success — I felt on top of the world, and those one-hundred-and-three women in my audience that day validated that belief. I was on my way. The old Peggy "I'm Scared" Parks was long gone. A confident businesswoman had emerged.

Let me now tell you about my business and the business of my business. The Parks Image Group, Inc. was born on April 1, 2004. I chose that start date just in case. If I failed, I could always say "April Fool's!"

Networking, I was told, was all-important, so I started visiting professional associations to see what it was about. I must have gone to every association in Atlanta. After a while, I decided to join Atlanta Women's Network; the members were a combination of corporate women (with whom I could identify) and entrepreneurs (with whom I hoped I could identify). I networked morning, noon, and night. Some evenings I was backing out of the driveway as my husband was coming home from work. Bernie was so supportive that I never realized how much I was neglecting him. After a while, though, I decided to attend evening events only if they were likely to be very productive. I still practice this.

I attended all the AICI Atlanta Chapter meetings, and one day our speaker was Lya Sorano, founder of Atlanta Women in Business. She invited our president, Sonya Barnes, to speak to her association. Sonya lives in Charlotte, North Carolina, and she turned around and said, "Well, since Peggy Parks lives here, why don't we have her represent us?" My heart stopped. I thought I was going to die. Oh, my gosh! How could Sonya expect me to represent AICI? I had just graduated from the London Image Institute, where she taught; she should have known I was petrified to speak in public!

A few months went by but, although I heard back from the organization's Executive Director, "our schedules were never compatible." When I could no longer say "no," I was booked to speak at a business club outside of Atlanta. What would I talk about? What would I wear? Could I keep my audience interested? I had so many doubts and fears.

Lya had asked me to speak for about forty-five minutes and an hour-and-a-half later, I was still answering questions. The next day I felt I had inadvertently overstayed my welcome and assumed those women had just been polite by staying longer than expected. That's how insecure I was. When I received a thank-you note from Lya stating that I had been so generous both in terms of the time I spent with the group and the valuable advice and tips I imparted, I was sure I had blown it. It took me a while to realize she meant what she said.

I now realize how well I did. I was hired by several of the guests and over time met some of the most amazing women in Atlanta. If it hadn't been for that group, I would have never met Angela Durden, who still remembers some of the tips and has put them into practice, and my two other co-authors, Marla and Eleanor. I also received many invitations to address other professional groups, and that's when I started feeling better about myself and learning about positive thinking. I was recruited for a TV appearance and a consulting arrangement with the program's host, booked for radio interviews, and given the opportunity to speak at a prominent national conference.

Had I not been a member of Atlanta Women in Business, those things may not have happened, certainly not so quickly, and with such a profound impact on the growth of my business.

When I started my business, I had never even heard of "networking." In the corporate world, I spent time with the people around me and did not think I needed to know anyone else. But for someone with a business of her own and a never-ending need to attract customers or clients, networking is indispensable. Even if the people you meet do not need your products or services, they know people who may — and when you build a relationship with them, they will be willing to make connections for you.

I still did not understand why people did not know what I knew. Many of them surprised me when they said, "Oh, I never thought of that." It was hard to admit I had a gift, an innate gift that I credit my mother and grandmother for. Not everyone, I discovered, has an eye for balance, color, style, scale, and proportion. As I always say, "Not everyone can know everything." Each of us has special talents; we cannot do or know it all.

Most of my speaking engagements were pro bono for the first two years. My hourly fee was very low compared with other image consultants' charges, but I never thought anyone would pay more. I kept being reminded that this was a business, not a hobby, but for a long time I felt I wasn't worthy. How can anyone expect to get paid when she's having so much fun?

Wow, it's really difficult starting your own business after twenty-five years in Corporate. I never had to go to HR and ask for my paycheck. It was always delivered on Fridays or deposited directly into my checking account. Finally, I raised my hourly fee by twenty-five dollars and people never questioned it. It took me another two years to add another twenty-five to my fee. Still no objection. This was crazy. I should have done it from the start, but I couldn't — I was paralyzed by fear. I was afraid people would think I was taking advantage of them.

Another thing I learned when I started my business is that other women entrepreneurs were willing to share advice and encouragement. All my life, women had been competition. We competed for men, for jobs, for whatever. I finally understood what Lya meant when she said, "If women don't support other women in the workplace, who will?"

It also became clear to me, almost immediately, that continuing education and certification are important. If your business operates in an industry that requires or encourages continuing education (real estate is a good example), you have to take advantage and keep adding those initials behind your name. This may not immediately bring you more business, but it will add to your credibility, which will get more prospects to take you seriously and inquire about your services.

My business has grown every year. I am making money and I am still having fun. What I have learned in the process are lessons every business owner must heed. A great deal of satisfaction comes from working with clients in the corporate world. Three in particular perfectly illustrate my work and exemplify the joy I experience in the services I provide. They are Rachel, Brad, and Kathryn (not their real names).

Rachel

One beautiful spring morning, I received an e-mail from a woman looking for someone to help her feel better about herself. She said she was in her early forties, worked for a financial services company, and felt old, frumpy, and tired. She never dressed for work, since there were only two people in her office, she and her manager. Clients did not visit, so she always came to the office in jeans and a shirt. Still, Rachel felt there was something missing in her life. Once we started a conversation, she kept talking about her manager, how she admired and looked up to her. She told me her manager was everything she wasn't: tall, thin, beautiful, and able to wear anything and look good. Rachel felt inferior.

After listening to her for a while, we set up an appointment to start with a closet organization. When I walked into her closet, I saw that most of her tops were fuchsia. I asked if that was her favorite color. She said it really wasn't, but it was her mother's favorite color and her mom had always bought her fuchsia clothes.

I had her try on the clothes, and we started making three piles: the "keep," the "needs to be altered," and the "don't think of wearing this again." A couple of hours later, the third pile was about three times bigger than the other two combined. Just about everything she owned was either too big, too small, the wrong color, or the wrong style. No wonder Rachel felt frumpy and old. She was a beautiful woman with thick light-brown hair, big hazel eyes, and gorgeous skin. But she did not put any emphasis on her attributes. Instead, she was hiding behind her clothes.

We had a great time working in her closet but encountered one problem — no clothes left to wear to the office the following Monday. That had never happened to me with a client because I always try to save as many clothes as possible by either having them altered or worn in different ways. I gave Rachel a shopping list and she went to the mall that evening to get a couple of things to wear until we could plan some formal shopping for her new core wardrobe.

Our next appointment was for a color analysis. Color, according to psychologists who have studied it, is the first thing one notices when meeting a person; its impact is immediate and lasting. Color affects your mood, apparent body shape, apparent age, outlook on life, and the overall impression you make. When you wear your best range of colors, you look energetic, vibrant, younger, and healthier. Amazing. Unflattering colors make you look ill, exhausted, dull, or older. Who needs that?

Rachel was typed as a Soft Autumn, meaning that she should wear warm tones, such as earth tones, beiges, browns, greens, and bronzes. The worst colors for a Soft Autumn are fuchsia and black. No wonder she thought she looked older than she was and could see only dark circles on her beautiful face!

Our next step was a style analysis. I like educating clients and giving them the tools they need to shop on their own and enjoy the experience. When I first started my business, I was shocked to find out that so many women hate shopping. They are overwhelmed when they walk into a department store. So many options, so many colors, so many styles! Once someone is taught her best colors and styles, it takes away a lot of stress, and she feels empowered to go straight to the garments that will flatter her.

With Rachel's vertical and horizontal body types determined, we were able to eliminate the clothes that would not flatter her. Off to the stores we went. We started with her core wardrobe: suits, jackets, pants, and skirts, all in basic earth tones, which looked beautiful on her. We chose underpinnings and accessories in brighter colors (no fuchsia), which showed off her beautiful hazel eyes that shift from blue to green, depending on the color she wears closest to her face.

Rachel continued mentioning her manager, but in a different way. It seemed that the manager was treating her differently, sometimes becoming rude or condescending. I was intrigued and wanted to meet this woman. I found an excuse to go to Rachel's office one day, knowing the manager would be there. It didn't take long to figure the woman out. She was the complete opposite of Rachel. She may have been tall and thin and well-dressed, but she was arrogant, rude, and patronizing. I, of course, was "the enemy." I had helped her subordinate bring out the essence of herself; now the manager felt threatened. She had noticed Rachel's metamorphosis but had never complimented her or said that she saw a change in her.

It has been such a joy to see Rachel blossom into the person she already was inside. Now when people meet her, they know she is a bright, beautiful, hardworking, successful woman with high values in life and a strong belief in her future.

A few years after meeting Rachel we made a date for lunch, and I picked her up at her office. She walked out of her building toward my car looking like a million dollars. Her posture was perfect; she had a smile on her face and walked as if she owned the world. I am so fortunate to have met her and helped her become on the outside the person she always was on the inside. There is nothing more rewarding than touching people's lives and helping them look better, feel better, and reach their life's goals more quickly.

Brad

When I first started my business, one of my friends who worked in a large company told all her friends and co-workers about me, almost becoming my unofficial PR agent. Her manager called one day and said she wanted me to work with one of her other employees. Brad had good skills and experience, but his manager thought he needed polishing. The company spends a lot of money on branding and is known globally. It encourages its employees to better themselves by providing them with personal and professional development services. It wants to make sure its employees represent the corporate brand well.

I was told this man was reticent, so I decided our first meeting should be over lunch, which would be somewhat casual and at the same time give me the opportunity to observe his table manners. I knew once he moved up the corporate ladder, which is what his manager expected, he would be entertaining clients. Did he know how to hold a fork and knife?

At first the conversation was strained; I had to pull every word out of him. His body language showed how uncomfortable he was, and I made sure I picked subjects that interested him. I had been told he loved music, so we talked about music, which was easy for me since my stepson is in the music business and I have learned a lot from him. Brad started relaxing and warming up to me.

When I returned to my office after our lunch, I sent a report to the manager who had brought me in. I told her that Brad needed better clothes (you always need to dress for your next job) and personal coaching on social graces: entertaining clients, how to pick a restaurant, how to pay the bill, how to make your guest feel special.

Brad and I worked together for about a year. We went shopping together, and I recommended a barber to keep his very curly hair in place. It looked as if his corporate career climb had received a significant boost.

A little more than a year after I finished my assignment with Brad, he called and told me he had quit his job and started a business. He was now a consultant with his own shop and needed my help once again.

This time he knew he needed to dress for his audience and have more than corporate clothes in his wardrobe. He also asked me to help with his Web site, business cards, logo, and marketing materials. By then he knew the value of consistency.

Once his Web site was up, he needed more visibility. Unless you tell people you are in business, they are not going to know. We decided which professional associations he should join and tried to find his specialty.

We then worked on branding strategies. When starting your own business, you will be more successful being an expert, a specialist, rather than a generalist. You need to focus on your niche. You cannot be everything to everyone or you will wind up being nothing to anyone. You need to know what your audience needs and learn how to meet those needs.

Be different from your competitors, whether it's your personality, the way you do business, or the way you offer your services.

People want to work with people with whom they can relate. Learn everything about the industry for which you want to be the expert: Track the trends, attend meetings, and read books and trade magazines. Subscribe to Google Alerts (www.google.com/alerts), which will keep you up to date on what's going on in your industry and with your competitors.

Self-promote. Brag is not a negative four-letter word, as Peggy Klaus tells us in *BRAG! The Art of Tooting Your Own Horn Without Blowing It*. There is a specific way of bragging and self-promoting. You cannot remain quiet about your accomplishments and expertise; however, you do not want to be labeled a braggart. Klaus recommends working on an elevator speech — a short pitch about your business, your awards, and your accomplishments that can be told in the time it takes an elevator to go from the lobby to the top floor or vice versa.

We talked about social media and what would work best for Brad. LinkedIn (www.linkedin.com) is the most professional; we posted his profile and recommendations came from past employers and current clients. We also uploaded PowerPoint presentations about his company and his services. Remember, though, that when you sign up for a presence on social media, you need to keep it up.

Be consistent. If you have a newsletter, send it out regularly, whether it's monthly, bi-monthly, or quarterly. The same applies to blogging. If you don't have time to blog every day or even every week, do it once a month. Your audience expects you to be consistent.

Your personality is also very important in self-branding. People want to do business with people who not only are like them but perhaps are also an improved version. People are attracted to people perceived as having it all together. No matter how well you know your clients, don't become their buddies. We have a tendency to let our guard down after we know our clients for a while and start talking too much about our personal lives, struggles, and challenges. They may listen, but subconsciously they wonder if you really still have it all together.

You need to be authentic, transparent, your true self. Do not be a hypocrite or try to be who you think your clients want you to be. You need to be consistent in all phases of your life. You cannot be one way in your public life and the opposite in your private life. The difference will eventually come out; there are no secrets anymore in this instant-communications world. Think of the scandals we hear about public figures and celebrities.

Kathryn

Kathryn, a high-level manager in a Fortune 500 company, called me one day. She had been in the same job for several years, and a friend had recommended me. She knew something was missing but could not quite figure out what. Although she managed about two-hundred employees, she did not feel she was getting the respect she should. She had twice been passed over for promotion. Growing up, she had always been told that if she did a good job people would notice. Apparently her company did not. She did not want to leave her job because she loved the company, but she wanted to move up in the corporate world. She felt stymied.

Her stay-at-home mother had always dressed in a very simple way and felt that girls and women who spent too much time on their looks were perceived as frivolous; what was important was education, being a good person, and treating others in a nice way. This is how Kathryn had been prepared for the world.

Kathryn dressed appropriately for her position in a corporate environment, but all her clothes looked the same. She wore a black or charcoal gray suit with a white blouse, black pumps, and suntan pantyhose — every day. She was a pretty woman in her mid-forties but looked older. She still dressed the way she had when she first entered the business world almost twenty years earlier. This made her look older and out of date. Her hair was nicely cut but was showing some gray. She put on lipstick in the morning but by lunchtime looked washed out.

Kathryn had a nice figure and was easy to dress. She could buy clothes off the rack with no need for alterations, which is unusual. However, she needed some punch to her dress. We updated her suits by adding color to her underpinnings. The white shirts and dark suits washed her out and made her look boring. Adding color close to her face brought attention to her face and made her look healthier and more vibrant. We also added a few accessories to her wardrobe, a couple of simple necklaces and scarves, plus shoes in colors other than black.

I also taught her how to take care of her skin. No matter how much makeup you wear, it will not make you look better unless you pay attention to your skin. Kathryn was showing lines around her eyes and mouth because she had spent quite a bit of time in the sun. It takes about twenty years for sun damage to show up on your skin. The good news is that it can be reversed. I put her on a maintenance skin care regimen and slowly added other products to make sure she got her cleaning/toning/moisturizing routine down pat before introducing products for the repair and prevention of further aging signs.

Once skin care became routine to her, I taught her how to wear makeup. She had always thought it would take thirty minutes to "put her face on," but we were able to do it in ten.

I then took her to my hairdresser, who added highlights around her face. I did not want Kathryn, who was not high maintenance, to need to go to the hairdresser every month to maintain her highlights. They blended nicely with her hair color and added a glow to her skin tone; a touch-up three or four times a year is all she needs.

After working with Kathryn, I received e-mails from her, telling me she was getting compliments, with some colleagues teasingly asking if she was in love. I could tell she was surprised because the subtle changes we made were not obvious to her, but she felt better about herself and was interacting with upper management more easily. She also had a new spring in her step.

What is the secret to success of this kind? Take baby steps. Had I tried to do a big makeover on Kathryn, she would have been overwhelmed and unable to follow my advice. We took baby steps in everything we did. I worked with her for eighteen months until we had the finished product, and I am happy to say that when we had lunch a few months later, she told me she had been promoted. She was on top of the world!

Perhaps the most beautiful result of working with clients like Rachel, Brad, and Kathryn, as well as many others, is the mutual benefit; sure, I help them make a more professional impression in the business world and feel better about themselves, but at the same time they add to my own self-confidence and joy in the work I have chosen to do. What more can a business owner hope for?

PEGGY PARKS'
RULES TO
A BETTER YOU

This chapter has given you insight into how I — late in life, some would say — evolved from an insecure, fearful employee into a confident business owner. It has given you a peek into the image world, and it has, I hope, given you tips and advice that you can carry into the business world, regardless of whether that is a career climb to the executive suite, ownership of a storefront on Main Street, or the presidency of a manufacturing plant in Asia. Let me end with these bottom line rules:

- Always dress for your next job.
- Zip up your adult suit when you walk out the door.
- Dress every day as if you were going to run into your ex.
- Fake it till you make it!
- Have confidence in yourself.

Peggy M. Parks
AICI CIP

The Parks Image Group, Inc. is an international image and etiquette consulting firm based in Atlanta, Georgia. It provides custom corporate workshops on professional business attire and etiquette, and private one-on-one consulting on image plans and wardrobe planning.

The Parks Image Group, Inc.

Post Office Box 52066 • Atlanta, Georgia 30355

www.TheParksImageGroup.com • (404) 266-3858

E-mail: Peggy@TheParksImageGroup.com
Blog: http://PeggyParks.Wordpress.com
Association of Image Consultants International (www.aici.org)
Atlanta Women in Business (www.atlantawomeninbusiness.com)
Georgia Association for Women Lawyers (www.gawl.org)

"I want to meet people
from whom I can learn more.
I want to meet and
surround myself with
people who have
a positive attitude."

Angela

Opportunities in Disguise

Angela K. Durden

www.AngelaDurden.com
www.MikeAndHisGrandpa.com

*"Angela, I need you to quit
school and get a job,"
my mother told me.*

It was a shock when my mother asked me, her oldest child, to quit school at sixteen so I could earn money to fund what she called "the very last time I will leave him" — her husband, my stepfather, our own family terrorist.

I loved school — it was my chance to be normal. I loved writing — it was my opportunity for escape. I loved words — I could control them.

When I wrote stories, teachers always chose mine to read aloud. Students, quiet and intent, never fidgeted. Often they turned to me — the quiet and always-new girl — as if to say, "She wrote that? Wow."

In fifth grade, the public librarian did not believe I read between ten and fifteen books every two weeks. She came to believe when she asked me what they were about and I could tell her.

However, as a dutiful daughter always fighting for my mother and siblings against that man, I didn't hesitate to quit school. Of course, my teachers and counselors were horrified. I could not tell them the truth. I had to come up with an answer that seemed plausible.

Although they knew I was lying and begged me to tell them what was really going on, I couldn't — for fear of death. My stepfather vowed he would kill us all if we left, so our plans had to remain top secret. It was a small, rural town in northeast Georgia; these well-meaning teachers and counselors might let the secret out.

My mother got me a full-time job in a cotton mill, six days a week from midnight to eight. For three-and-a-half years I was a spinner, a cloth inspector, and a cloth grader. During the night I can still sometimes smell the raw cotton. The memory of that scent is so powerful, all the memories and feelings of that time rush back in on me anew.

Within a year of my quitting school, though, Mom gave birth to her third son and fifth child. Our plan to leave was put on hold.

During the next two-and-a-half years, I worked and paid many of the family bills, bought the family groceries, and paid for most of the clothes for my sister and three brothers. I also was told I would purchase a car, and then I was in hock to the used car lot owner for two years.

Not a penny was saved for The Great Escape.

At nineteen, I decided to get my general education degree from the State of Georgia. I didn't have time to study for it — I was working six nights a week — so I decided to take my chances and took the two-day test. Within a couple of months I received a letter informing me I passed and that the diploma would be sent. I still have the letter, but the diploma never arrived.

In the Spring of 1977, Mom was ready to leave her man. She asked me to move out of state in preparation. In the Autumn of that year, Mom finally left and joined me in North Carolina. She and my three brothers were with me for only one week before her husband tracked her down. They had a tearfully emotional reunion, and she and the boys returned to their own hell.

Shortly thereafter, my sister and I returned to Georgia, where I met the man who would become my husband. Compared to most of the men I had met, L.H. was a godsend.

Before we married, he made sure I got home safely from work each night. When he came for dinner, he helped with the dishes. He had just started a business, the first of three. He was divorced, had no children, and after six years of service had been honorably discharged from the Air Force. Compared to my family, his looked like the Nelsons and the Cleavers rolled into one.

He smiled at me and spoke politely. He was helpful to my friends and family. He seemed to know a lot about almost everything. He spoke pleasantly and confidently with a variety of people. L.H. had a great sense of humor and told jokes that made me laugh.

What wasn't there to like? This was a man I could learn from. I envisioned a great lifelong partnership.

My life was looking up.

He wanted me to work when we got married; I was all for that. But, hey, you play, you pay; naturally I got pregnant. He wanted me to be a stay-at-home mom. I was all for that, too; so I did. I was going to be the best mom and wife I could be; my children would never suffer as I had, and I would give my husband a wife he could be proud of.

I was eager to learn all I could about being a good wife and mother and set my mind and heart to becoming them.

But I was also keen to learn about business. My father-in-law subscribed to *The Wall Street Journal* and *Forbes*. Each visit to his house would find me deep into reading back issues. He would not throw them away until I had read them. Later he gave me a subscription to *Forbes*. What a treat! Even though the subscription was in my husband's name, I didn't care; I knew it was for me and I would be the only one reading it.

That was how I educated myself on the ins and outs of business during my first fifteen years of marriage. I did not always understand what I was reading, but I became familiar with the language of business as well as industry types and the people who made it happen or who failed spectacularly only to rise from the ashes of financial ruin. I particularly liked the stories of those who failed but tried again.

During that time my husband started his second and third businesses. Of course I wanted to help him grow them, often suggesting marketing ideas. He refused my ideas, but was unable to stifle my passion for business.

I kept the books and paid the bills for his businesses, but he did not pay me, even though our accountant told him about the tax advantages. Asked why, L.H. told the accountant, "Because she'll just blow the money." My feelings were hurt by his attitude, but no more conversation was allowed.

In any case, I was a highly frustrated marketing machine.

Just before our tenth anniversary, I wrote a story about a traveling circus that came to our town of Toccoa, Georgia, and showed it to a friend.

She said, "Angela, you must submit this to the newspaper."

I'd never thought of submitting it, but I went to the offices of *The Chieftain* after closing time and dropped it into the mail slot. The next day the editor asked where I got the story. Did he think I stole it?

"I wrote it," I told him firmly.

"You wrote it? Can you come see me?"

I did, and the newspaper promptly hired me as a freelancer. I wasted no time searching out special-interest stories, not only writing about some great people but also illustrating the stories with my own photos.

From that point, no matter where I went in the county, I never had to show my driver's license when I wrote a check. People knew me from my picture in the newspaper. Of far greater importance to me, everyone loved the stories I wrote. As a bonus, my father-in-law couldn't have been happier; my success and good reputation spilled over to him. Thus the seed was sown that maybe — just maybe — I could make a little money by writing. The harvesting of that realization was a long way off.

When my two children were in school, I became a substitute teacher. After all, in my mind I was still a stay-at-home mom. But there came a time when I was no longer satisfied with simply learning about marketing and business and the business of writing. I wanted to practice what I'd learned.

More importantly, I wanted to have some say-so in the financial decisions of the marriage, which my husband said would happen only when I brought in some real money. Substitute teaching did not bring in enough for a chip in that game.

But where, when, and how could I earn more?

I figured the best way was to start a business, but L.H. forbade me. By then, however, my mind needed the stimulation, my ego the boost, and my pocketbook the green; I went forward with my plans.

L.H. asked what I was planning to do with the money. That comment should have cheered me because he obviously thought I was going to make decent money. He thought I would be keeping it to spend as I wished. After assuring him the money would be going toward the family, he reluctantly gave me the go-ahead.

By this time, though, I was not looking for his permission.

But why did I think I could sell my writing skills and parlay them into a company offering marketing, printing, and layout and design services?

How did I come to believe that I could offer consulting services?

Or manage manufacturers' validation processes for heavy equipment dealerships to prove they were properly representing the product in the marketplace, meeting sales expectations, and otherwise operating their businesses profitably?

Or, among other things, set up a publishing company?

How did I, a stay-at-home mom with no business, management, or technical experience, end up starting a small business?

Truthfully, I never saw myself doing any of those things, because other than the writing, I didn't know they existed. My customers asked more of me; it was they who thought I could do those things.

But what motivated the initial change in my attitude fifteen years into my marriage? What made me choose a course that from the very start solidly pitted me against the very husband I had previously been happy, eager, and willing to partner with in every way?

I had heard it said that until a person is in a huge amount of pain, she will not do anything to alter her circumstances. In other words, she has to hit rock bottom before she can go up. Until then, I didn't understand.

I finally did. I had emotionally and mentally hit that bottom rock. No longer could I go into a classroom; when I saw a girl who resembled me as a young child, I had vivid flashbacks of abuse. I couldn't go to work because L.H. wouldn't like any intrusion that might breach our orderly schedule.

What was left? Starting my own business, of course, where I could have complete control of my schedule.

I had made some money writing. I knew I was good at it. When we moved back to Atlanta from Toccoa, I was offered a job with *The Atlanta Journal-Constitution* based upon my writings for *The Chieftain*. Problem was the job was full-time, which would have greatly conflicted with my children's school schedule and my husband's requirements.

Another venue I explored was freelancing. I sold a couple of articles to national trade magazines and newsletters and another to *Atlanta Parent*. This method did not prove to be a source for the income I wanted to generate.

Further research told me I should focus on small business. The market was underserved, which was ideal for me. I chose a name for my business — WRITER for HIRE! — and off I went to get my business license.

That name looked good on the license. The pride I felt upon getting it was immense — and the fear equaled the pride.

Becoming True to My Vision

When I opened WRITER for HIRE!, my idea and my husband's idea of what it would be were worlds apart. L.H. did not understand what I wanted to do and did not know there was a market for it. All he could wrap his mind around was that I would type for businesses and help people organize their resumes. When he made the sign to put at the mailbox, it read:

TYPING

and

RESUMES

We arrived at that witty bit of self-promotion after a couple of days of arguing about what my sign would say. I gave up when I saw the blank and uncomprehending look in L.H.'s eyes. The customers I wanted weren't going to ride by my house, so I shut up, said thank you, and the sign went up.

I found my first customers by going business to business, introducing myself, and leaving a business card. This approach was modestly successful. In my second year, though, I became more focused on business segments, or types, so I could leverage the information I gained from research and write the same letter many times over, instead of having to formulate many.

How I happened to choose car dealerships I do not remember, but it seemed like a good idea. I identified eight dealerships and made phone calls to get each general manager's name. I crafted a letter to each and sent them off. To hold myself accountable for following up, I promised I would be calling them within a few days.

Within two hours of making my promised calls, I had gained three face-to-face appointments and subsequently added one customer, a Chrysler-Jeep dealership, which I retained for four years until CarMax bought out their franchises.

Even this customer came after a hard sell. During my initial meeting with the general manager, he told me he was looking for someone who could do several things:

Could I take all their customer logs and input names, addresses, and phone numbers into a database? *Absolutely.*

Could I design, lay out, write, and print a quarterly customer-focused newsletter with coupon inserts? *Sure. I can handle it.*

Using a database, could I prepare and mail the newsletters and coupon? *Sure. Anything else?*

No, that was the whole project. How much would that cost me? *I need to do some research and get some final numbers and get back with you.*

In the meantime, the GM said he had a consultant working with the dealership who would like to meet with me in a couple of days. *Be happy to.*

The date was set, we shook on it, and I walked confidently to my vehicle. About two miles down the road I completely freaked out.

What the heck is a database?

Newsletter layout and design?

Bulk mail fulfillment?

I had a vague idea of all of these things, but vague did not mean I could do it. And there was the small matter of my husband. I had not mentioned any of my plans to him. L.H. did not know about my meetings, and he certainly had no idea about my assurances to this new customer.

Again, I kept my mouth shut.

The next day I was at the library (these were infant Internet and home computer days) finding out everything I could about databases and methods for producing layout and design. By the time I left I had simplified the problem, identified other resources I could call upon, understood the pros and cons of various database-management systems, and was familiar with the top brand names.

I also went to see the printer who had done a few small jobs for me and told her what the project would entail, at least as close as I could figure.

The following day I arrived early for my appointment with the GM and his high-priced consultant. As I was shown into his office, the consultant was sitting quite comfortably and looking confident. Immediately I was overcome with fear.

Who did I think I was?

But in a take-charge manner, I put on a happy face and confidently shook hands all around. I, too, sat comfortably.

The discussion lasted almost an hour. The consultant threw questions at me right and left, the most pressing of which were about the database system I planned to use for this most-important project for his most-important customer. He was trying to get me to commit to a particular brand that was in popular usage at the time.

Mind you, I had never used a computer; it was 1993, after all. I did not know the difference between hardware and software.

However, my fast research had been exhaustive and indicated the particular program the consultant was promoting was full of quirky bugs and was based on unstable program code, which not only produced unreliable data but made it very difficult to use. My research had also indicated which type, not brand, of simplified database system could be used to better effect.

Several times I attempted to answer the consultant in such a way I would not hurt his feelings while allowing him to come to the conclusion he was misinformed. He didn't get the hint, nor did he take the opportunity to save face, and he kept pressing me on it.

"Fine. Let me tell you what I do know," I told him politely, but in a take-no-prisoners manner.

Facts were quoted, sources cited as basis, accurate conclusions stated. The GM hid a smile and the consultant shut up. A mail date was set. I left the dealership with piles of customer logs ready for input.

Input — a word I did not yet know.

If I thought I was freaked out two days before, I was truly freaked out now. My research showed that to accomplish all I said I could do, I needed a computer, and more. At the time, ordinary people like me didn't have home computers. My recipes were written on paper and sat conveniently on the shelf. I noticed the warehouse club, of which I was a member, had personal computers. I spent the next two days doing more exhaustive research.

What type of computer did I need to do all these types of projects?

RAM and ROM and hard drive megabytes and floppy drives and Mac or Windows and software and hardware and monitors and cables and printers and labels…oh, my.

Not only that, what was the cost? I almost fainted.

The system and everything else I needed would eat up almost the entire net profit I had made the year before. Until that time, the most I had ever put on a credit card was two-hundred-and-fifty dollars — my husband almost had a meltdown.

Can you see the pressure I was under? I didn't want to upset L.H., but I wanted to grow my business. I pulled out the credit card and within three days had everything needed. Now it was my husband who was freaking out. It does not matter the conversational details about what he considered another rebellion against his authority. What does matter is that I had made up my mind to act like a business owner and take that step.

When L.H. had been in business, he invested in tools and technology — oftentimes when we could least afford it — that would allow him to make more money while saving time, thus effectively increasing his profit margin. He explained to me how the expenditure made economic sense. That position was reasonable, and I never disagreed or made an issue of it.

Therefore, in the back of my mind, I hoped and prayed L.H. would understand. But he didn't. He made a big issue of the purchase, and day after day I heard about it. But my customer was counting on me and I was not going to let him down. My ego was on the line. My pride in myself could not afford any more hits. I had given my word.

Two months later, when the project was delivered and I presented my invoice for several thousand dollars, the GM never blinked.

I couldn't get to the bank fast enough to deposit that check. When it cleared, I paid my commercial printer and nailed the credit card bill in full. Only then could I breathe and sleep again.

I netted two-thousand dollars, and the next project due date had been set. L.H. now understood there was a market for what I wanted to do. Any issue he had went away. He clapped his hands and said, "It's all gravy now!"

His basic attitude remained the same, though. We had another disagreement when I had to upgrade my computer. It didn't last as long, but I had to wonder why I was having the same conversation again.

The Value of a Good First Impression

Two years after I sent out my first letters to the car dealerships, I received a call from a salesperson at a dealership previously contacted with no success. The general sales manager had been given my information and was told to call me, which resulted in another long-term customer. It had been so long since my original contact that I had completely forgotten about them.

All of which reinforces my belief that you should never underestimate the value of a personal touch — a well-written introductory letter, with business card inserted, and the promise of phone follow-up. I had made such a good first impression that I earned another customer two years after the fact. I make this point because nowadays people undervalue letters personally written, sent in an envelope, and having an actual stamp. I still use this method, and it still works — more so now than ever in this day of poorly written, badly formatted, and often misspelled e-mails full of politically correct phrasing and buzzwords often misused.

Never underestimate the power of language used well and the pleasing placement of that language on a piece of paper.

Assumptions

"Angela, we have decided to go with another company."

These words were said in my seventh year in business by a man who truly liked me and appreciated what I had done for his company. It was obvious from the pained look on his face that he did not want to have this conversation. But I had brought about this response because of an error in judgment — I had made the assumption that because he was happy each time I delivered, he would always be happy with what I delivered.

He probably would have been happy had I not compounded the problem with another false assumption: I had assumed no one else was after his business or could offer him anything better.

He had chosen me for this long-term marketing assignment. I had handled it for almost three years and made his company look good, allowing him to stand out from his competitors.

But when he compared what I had to offer with what my competition offered, he could see I had not been keeping up with the times. To his bosses he looked incompetent. I had let him down.

I continued to do a few projects for this customer on a lesser level for another year or so. But there came a time when their industry had a radical and worldwide shift, severely cutting marketing dollars. After an explanation, which he did not owe me, I was informed I was no longer needed at all.

On the one hand, I was devastated and my ego took a huge hit. My self-worth was seriously questioned and what knowledge I did possess was on shaky ground. After all, wasn't I missing the resources necessary to compete against all these great companies with up-to-date technology and a highly trained staff and flashy sales force?

I did not try to find new business to replace what I had lost. I was content to let my business simply wither away. I would service what remaining customers I had until they, too, discovered I didn't have my act together and chose not to call me again.

On the other hand, I knew I had this loss coming. For previous employers I had always looked at the challenges presented, often identifying challenges they had not seen. How could performance be improved? Where could efficiency measures be implemented to save time and increase production?

I knew I was capable of performing at a much higher level.

Assumptions — not always the best thing to rely upon when making business decisions. So what were these bad business decisions that resulted in my being fired in the seventh year in business?

Pure Madness

The first and foremost bad business decision was resting upon my own laurels, also known as laziness. I chose to believe that what my customer told me ("Great job, Angela!") and the fact the check cleared meant I was constantly performing at peak.

A very close second was my desire to pocket most of the money and not put it into improvements. I didn't reinvest in up-to-date technology or learn how to use it; nor did I keep up with where my industry was going or what my competition was doing.

"How," I asked myself despondently, "did I allow myself to fall into this state of mind?"

Even knowing I would get grief for it only two years into business, I had invested thousands of dollars in a computer system, peripherals, and specific software, and learned how to use these to best benefit because I knew such equipment was necessary to properly service the customers I truly wanted.

One of my mistakes was believing what I had and what I knew was enough to ensure success — which was pure madness. I had assumed that no one else was after my customers' business or could offer them anything better. Of course, this line of thinking left my company vulnerable in the war for the customer's checkbook.

My thinking was shaped, in large part, by my desire to use good business manners. Well-mannered folks, I erroneously thought, did not steal customers. Yes — they can, they will, and they do.

Further, they will smile while they do it. All customers are fair game.

I thought if a company accepted me as a vendor or service provider, that meant no one else prior to my arrival had ever been hired by this company to do this particular job. It never dawned on me the reason I may have been chosen was because someone else wasn't doing a good job.

You might say I was successful in spite of myself. I made some good decisions at first, then stagnated on several levels being content with the status quo, developing some odd ideas about how business really worked, and deciding I was not really ever going to make much money.

Losing this customer only proved I was right in my assumptions. (There is that nasty word again.)

However, I have never been one to wallow for long or allow myself completely to give in to negative thoughts. Soon I became aware that another customer's business was growing.

Licking My Wounds

I met the Adams brothers in 1992, my first year in business. They had a cubbyhole for an office and shared a bathroom with another company. I told them I could write their quotation letters and properly format them on their letterhead. All they would have to do was sign, then fax or mail. Tony was dead set against hiring me because he wanted to keep his money in his pocket and thought my services would not benefit them.

His thinking closely mirrored my own thoughts about investing in my company. I saw where he was wrong, yet was blind to my own condition.

The other brother, Buddy, insisted otherwise, thank goodness. I tried to become invisible in their cramped space while listening to them argue vehemently for their respective positions about the value of my services.

"Well, I am the president and I'm overriding you," said Buddy, and that was the end of that discussion — at least while I was there. I left the office with a couple of quotations to type; I had my second customer.

Five years later they had hired three men and purchased two more Class 8 commercial trucks, another huge forklift, and two more specialized hauling trailers. They were now doing well enough that they could afford to move into their own spacious building, complete with offices, warehouse, two bathrooms, and a break room.

So, here I was, in year seven, upset about losing this other customer, still writing quotations for the brothers, when they telephoned and said, "Angela, we need some help. Come see us." They were in dire need of someone to properly set up an office, improve their bookkeeping practices, upgrade their computers, and handle invoicing, paying bills, and processing payroll.

This lasted almost two years and suited me at the time. I needed to feel a sense of accomplishment in tackling a large project while still being able to give myself time to think about where I really wanted to take my business.

I found that playing at working for someone else was not what I wanted. The brothers took it very badly when I told them they needed to find a full-time person.

Although they felt I let them down, I knew I was not what they needed. How did I know? Because I was bored to tears. There was no more challenge. I began to loathe the idea of going into that office and doing that work, even just two or three days a week. I had been keeping my eyes open for opportunities to expand my own business. By now I had figured out where I wanted my business to go.

So about the time I fired my customer (talk about a switch in my thinking), I had already taken on a larger company in addition to my smaller and regular customers.

This new customer was, and still is, a well-known and respected regional car and commercial truck dealer group in Atlanta. I handled customer contact via a marketing newsletter for the wholesale parts department. When an investment firm told them they needed to get print costs in line with industry standards, the only person they had regular contact with in that trade was me.

As I gathered their forms and compared their vendor and dealership pricing levels, I was in a prime spot to learn all about my competitors.

That information allowed my business to grow quickly.

When I visited each of my customer's locations — and learned about the company for the marketing project, gathered their print costs data and interpreted the meaning of that data for them — I identified opportunities for more business with the company.

Three years later I was doing business with each location and division, and the president always took my calls.

Heady times. Ego felt really good. I was laughing loud and walking tall.

Challenges

Then came a challenge, one that nearly ruined me. I almost cut my own throat financially.

Because I still believed that in the long run I was not going to be successful, I did not charge what I was worth. Often I performed — at no charge — tasks not contracted for. People came to expect these things and I gladly did them without telling them I was doing it.

I wasn't going broke, but I wasn't making much of a profit, either. My goodness, the money I could have made. Makes me sick to think about it.

The second challenge, one that completely blindsided me, came when the dealer group — now almost twice the size it was when they first became my customer — was bought by an NYSE-traded company with a national footprint. All of a sudden there were tensions and a corporate mindset that had not existed in this previously privately owned company. Everything was changing, and all the changes seemed to have a negative impact on me as well as faithful and long-term employees. Even the president didn't have the same authority as before.

Prior to the corporate takeover, only the variable (sales) side of the business had high turnover, typical for the car business. But now the fixed (parts and service) side was losing loyal and key employees, some of whom had been with the company fifteen or more years.

Everybody was watching their backs.

Having no patience for office politics and the posturing and strutting of huge egos, I now know I could have better handled my interactions with the new faces. Maybe not always, but more than was needed, I turned the company's changes into a personal attack against me. Granted, some of it truly was personal and petty, but had I handled it differently, I would have been able to weather the storm much better.

I did weather it, and the company is still a customer — just a different and constantly changing one.

This highlights another assumption on my part — that my customers would always remain the same.

I, like most people, do not like change. But when a comfort zone is inhabited blindly, customers and business suffer.

When I was at my lowest point, I attended a business conference where two women independently gave me pieces of advice.

"If you want to be a CEO, start acting like one," one told me.

"If you want to be valued, stop working for cheap or free," said the other.

The drive home that evening was unpleasant; I cried the whole way. But there were also some positives. By the time I pulled into the driveway, I was putting together those two pieces of advice and my plan was in place.

The old woe-is-me-I-ain't-worth-a-dime attitude was gone. (Let me say it often tries to rear its old, ugly head, but I give it a good slap and it hides again for a while.)

I became WBENC-certified (Women's Business Enterprise National Council, www.wbenc.org). I looked for more business, and it came my way. Profits rose and my customers were not complaining about the increases for my services.

Watching my costs became an operational standard, not the loosey-goosey affair it had been. I confirmed estimates and quotes, and included enough hours, all materials for the job, and enough profit to cover overhead and still make a living — plus a little cushion.

I was also able to sit in on several yearly business planning meetings for both dealers and the manufacturers they represented. There I learned my customers do not absorb the costs of doing business. They pass costs along to their customers.

I put this operational standard into practice, too.

I didn't realize it right away, but the change in my internal attitude was being felt, if not outright noticed, by many people. During this time several opportunities came my way to significantly grow my business.

First of all, I was tempted to borrow money to invest in a prominent location, hire a staff, and obtain pre-press equipment. I had already picked out a location and had quotes for equipment, plus customers were lined up and ready to jump onboard. I even had a business plan.

My second opportunity was equally as daring. I was approached privately by one of my vendors, the ready-to-retire owner of a well-established and respected printing firm who wanted me to purchase his company. We had often talked about the challenges we were facing and brainstormed through problem-solving sessions. My input, he said, helped him solve some thorny employee, production, and marketing issues.

It was a nice-looking fit. We had the same ownership visions and objectives, plus he knew his long-term employees would be safe.

The last opportunity came when another vendor, who had previously been a partner at a large printing company but was now on his own, approached me about going into business with him — as equal partners — to start our own printing and marketing company. We also had discussed many business challenges and found solutions for them.

Each was tempting and had its upside. But each would require that scariest of all business propositions — creative financing.

To grow these companies quickly — and fast growth would have been required at those levels — I would have to mortgage the house and/or max out the credit cards.

I had to do some real soul-searching. But when push came to shove, there was one thing I knew I needed every night and that was sleep. Could I sleep knowing everything I had was collateral and that I had thousands and thousands of dollars tied up in unsecured credit card debt? The answer was a loud and resounding "No."

These opportunities came at a time when people thought nothing of financing business opportunities and/or growth by taking out second and third mortgages on their houses — their homes where their children lived! — and living on credit cards.

"Oh, Angela, it's wonderful. The payoff is going to be great!" they said.

"Are you sleeping at night?" I asked.

"No. But that's a small sacrifice. You see, my house is going to increase in value year after year, and then I'm going to be able to pay off everything and the business will be up and running great by then and…" they continued, often with details of college savings for the kids and retirement plans.

Great goals. Bad methodology.

"No tenant left behind" loan policies forced on banks by power-seeking community activists led to the sub-prime mortgage meltdown.

People "flipped that house" into financial oblivion.

Investment houses closed, banks weakened or failed, and the largest U.S. Chevrolet mega-dealer with a national footprint went toes up.

All of this because of what? Creative financing. Also known as taking the shortcut and the easy way.

My worry level is very low. More to the point, compared to many who called my decisions naiveté and chuckled at my earlier hesitancy to "be bold" or "make an investment in my dream," my financial foundation is very stable. The four-page fastest-growing-company-in-America article in *Inc.* or *Forbes* will not be about me.

Of course, I will not turn down an article should either publication want to write one. But fast growth, millions in debt, and investor relations are, I have discovered, not for me.

I will not chase a dream without a very solid plan. And I will not put my house up for that dream nor will I throw money at it.

These are my business decisions which afford me the opportunity to make decent profits with minimal stress. They also allow me to maintain solvency, plus the freedom to pursue other life goals. My business supports my life — not the other way around.

I am confident in my decisions and feel assured enough that I don't have to prove anything to anyone. Especially if it means risky financial choices.

In short, I have learned to say no without feeling the need to explain it to anyone's satisfaction or asking their approval.

On the other hand, I don't want to be stupid and throw away business opportunities. There came a point where my workload was so heavy that I was working around the clock. I made arrangements to handle the load by hiring a part-time assistant.

I was also having fun, even if I was tired.

Will the Challenges Never End?

Admittedly, I made more trouble for myself than I really needed by allowing L.H.'s input into the running of a business he did not understand. In my desire to make him feel needed, I often shared some of the challenges, problems, or issues I was encountering with vendors, jobs, or customers.

Not a bad thing to do with a husband.

In hindsight, however, I was sharing in such a way as to make him want to protect me and fix the problem. When he made a suggestion that did not fit and I didn't accept his advice, he got mad because he felt rejected. Then I got mad because he was treating me like an immature girl and the cycle would continue.

Had I acted like a mature businesswoman capable of solving problems instead of a helpless girl who needed saving, we could have been spared some negative discourse.

The bottom line: I acted helpless because I was trying to relieve his discomfort at having a wife who not only was growing and changing, but one who also was becoming respected outside the home.

Over the years I have had many conversations with women who have said their husbands did not want them to work outside the home, start a business, or do anything that would cause them to go outside the sphere of their husband's influence.

Often husbands are afraid their wives will leave them because they assume they won't be needed anymore.

All of these women agreed on one thing — instead of their husbands' behavior bringing them closer together, it drove the wives further away. It's a vicious and circular fear-based cycle that does not have a happy outcome.

Profit Defined

I was able to start my business and operate profitably from day one because my office was in my home. I offered services requiring no investment in stock or product.

But keep in mind that my profit was enhanced by the fact I did not have to pay the household bills. My husband's job supported us. My business was a means for generating cushion money — funds that would eliminate our debt more quickly, or that would allow us to go on vacation and to dine out instead of my cooking all our meals in a kitchenette. I made enough money we were able to pay off the house twelve years early, too. Something I was proud of and surprised my husband with.

My first year in part-time business, I netted over five-thousand dollars. That may not sound like much now, but at the time that was the best money I had ever earned. Why?

Because I made it based upon my own power — my own thoughts, my own effort. I found the customers. I came up with the ideas.

I did it.

Me.

That I earned it all working part-time hours made me even happier.

Nevertheless, if I had to support the family on that, it's obvious I would not have been able to do it. I recommend starting a business in this fashion because the heavy financial pressure is off. I was able to be the stay-at-home mom I wanted to be and earn more money in a shorter period than a regular part-time job would have allowed.

Of course, the more I made, the more I realized I could make — and my competitiveness kicked in. I enjoy making more than I ever thought possible on my own. I enjoy learning and applying that knowledge to better affect my bottom line.

The Future

I have neither a long-term business plan nor a grand vision. I am not going to build my company into a multi-million-dollar venture nor will I have employees.

Sure, I want to make money. But it's more important to me to keep my options open — completely. I want to meet people from whom I can learn more. I want to have many new life and business experiences. I want to meet and surround myself with people who have a positive attitude. I want to minimize contact with — or completely keep out of my life and business — all evil creeps, user-jerks, jackasses, and negativity junkies.

A tall order, I know.

How I will make money is not set in stone and that scares me.

I grew up the oldest of five children immersed in a violent and out-of-control home — a home filled with daily life-and-death situations, of which I was often caught in the middle while trying to save someone. I saw my mother waitress in restaurants and bars, deliver newspapers, work in cotton mills, clean houses, and more, to earn money. I saw her pay off debts that were not hers. When her hard-earned money was stolen by her husband, I heard her beg the bill collectors: "Please come and find all my hidden money; please, because I can't find it."

The Repo Man was a frequent visitor to my childhood homes, as were the police, pedophiles, junkies, and criminals of all types.

There was no such thing as a savings account.

There was no understanding of how business and money worked.

There was no planning.

There was no talk of the future because we didn't have the luxury of thinking about it.

There was no opportunity for a higher education — although what I did learn, I learned well and hard. I lived that way for a long, long time.

Fear kept me from expanding my horizons.

Fear kept me bound by situations that were uncomfortable, at best, and downright awful, at worst.

Fear kept me in a marriage longer than necessary.

Fear made me accept the negatives others thrust upon me.

Fear let others dictate my life's decisions.

Finally, it was fear that forced me to change my life.

The fear of living with the negative — or, rather, living without the positive. Yes, indeed, these fears were the catalyst for my taking the plunge and going into business. And it was through this process that other positive changes in my life came about. I have now published several of my own books, selling enough of them to break even with the promise of more sales and more opportunities to come.

I have used my first children's book as a platform for paid speaking gigs, for professional advancement, and in schools where I share my passion and love of the proper, creative, and fun use of words.

And what have I learned about myself and about business?

I can go into many different industries and do well because I can and am willing to learn.

I can step outside my comfort zone and tackle something unknown to me and succeed.

I can fail and keep going and get better.

There are all sorts of jobs out there and I can do many of them.

If I don't let my ego dictate the type of job I look at, if I do everything asked of me — as long as it is not illegal, immoral, or will make me fat — better things will come my way.

Better things usually equate to more money and opportunities.

Once upon a time I took for granted that if I stayed within my comfort zone, life would never change. I was wrong.

But now I have options. I never before knew I had options.

I love options.

I also love individuals who can help me identify and take advantage of those options.

I love people who can inspire me to be a better me and who are not only happy for me when I try-and-do, or when I try-and-fail, but mainly are simply happy I tried.

Once upon a time I thought I had to stand alone against the negative forces this world thrust upon me. Again, I was wrong.

I now know I can ask for help.

I love knowing I don't have to rely solely upon myself.

I love knowing I have people I can go to for advice.

I love those who know, understand, and believe that, even in failure, I am still a good person — and that I am quite capable of navigating the murky waters of change.

Without a doubt, I most certainly don't like those waters. But I am no longer paralyzed by fear of the unknown.

ORGANIZATIONS:

Atlanta Women in Business (www.atlantawomeninbusiness.com)

Atlanta Chapter President, National Association of Professional Women (www.napw.com)

National Association of Women Business Owners (www.nawbo.org)

Truck Writers of North America (www.twna.org)

Angela K. Durden

WRITER for HIRE! helps businesses use words to best represent them. We pick the words, place them on paper, and produce them. By working together, the story of the business is told creatively and warmly. Graphic design and print brokering added to the words makes this a comprehensive solution for marketing, advertising, and print needs.

WRITER for HIRE! Press provides publishing services ranging from coaching and editing to design, layout, and production.

WRITER for HIRE! and WRITER for HIRE! Press
1740 Hudson Bridge Road • Suite 1209
Stockbridge, Georgia 30281
angeladurden@msn.com • (770) 898-6950
www.AngelaDurden.com • www.MikeAndHisGrandpa.com

"The legacy of a person rests
not in things but
in the people whose lives
have been enriched by
their willingness
to care."

Eleanor

Dreams
Realized

Eleanor Morgan

www.MDECorps.com
www.ClaritySpecialists.com

When I think about it,
I believe my life could have
been the basis for a hit
TV show — or two.

While my childhood fulfilled the images of such programs as *Father Knows Best*, I grew up to become something far less typical — more like *The Mary Tyler Moore Show* or *Murphy Brown*. These strong, smart women overcame stereotypes to prove themselves as professionals in their own right. Like them, I followed my own vision, but I went into business when such businesswomen were the exception rather than the rule.

I grew up the oldest of three in a middle class neighborhood in Birmingham, Alabama. My father, Walton, was serving in the Air Force the year I was born, and later applied the skills he learned there to his civilian career as an aircraft mechanic for Hayes Aircraft Corp. My mother, Jean, had few choices in a work world reserved for men, but she was an excellent CEO of our home.

Everything in my little world was a walk or a bike ride away. I played and pretended and happily wasted time on weekends during the school year and during the hot, lazy summer months. My favorite destination was the library, a magnificent old building where I could indulge my passion for exploring worlds beyond my own and soak up the knowledge I craved.

As I grew older, though, my mind grew more attuned to the adult world and its concerns. Labor strikes affected my dad's employment. Every time there was a strike, Dad would find a temporary job, sometimes driving a milk truck in the dim early mornings or toiling as a sanitation worker. There may have been questions of where the money would come from, but never a doubt that he would somehow take care of us.

When I graduated from high school, my parents didn't have the money for college tuition, and I was too naïve to know of other options available to finance higher education. So I went to work typing insurance policies and other documents for an underwriting company. The experience turned me into a skilled typist, at the time quite a valuable ability for a career woman.

Forming the Dream

I have a memory of one special person who affected me early and whose influence has lasted to this day. Her name was Miss Polly and she lived across the street. My destiny was set from the moment my six-year-old eyes caught a glimpse of this business school graduate in her smart, dark flannel skirt; off-white, short-sleeved sweater; and tall, tall black heels. That vision ignited ambition and inspired a vow:

I would be a businesswoman.

Miss Polly's daily comings and goings seasoned my childhood with tantalizing peeks into what I imagined was the sophisticated, glamorous life of the business world and the women who inhabited it. Luckily, our relationship was not one-sided.

Miss Polly married; they became the owners of a firm that repaired large equipment. With her knowledge of bookkeeping, Miss Polly handled the finances and ran the office; her husband managed operations and strategy.

A year after I began working in underwriting, I accepted a job offer from Miss Polly, who promptly took me under her wing. She shared their expertise on business and gave me many opportunities to get to know every aspect. She knew ambition burned in my brain and took every chance to fuel that flame. I, too, wanted to make decisions and help other people be successful — just as Miss Polly was helping me.

Working Toward the Dream

My vow to become a businesswoman, made with the earnestness and simple certainty of childhood, has been fulfilled. I am president and CEO of Atlanta-based MD&E, Inc., a company my husband and I own. We grew MD&E from a vision into an eight-million-dollar organization with a staff of more than eighty. MD&E provides professional services, project management, and long-term tactical business support to midsized and Fortune 500 companies through system data support.

I would like to say there came a point early on where I had the grand vision of the business and never wavered from fulfilling it. In truth, the journey was more like going through the fun house at the county fair — feeling my way around life's experiences, bumping into some barriers, and getting a few surprises along the way. I looked for openings and opportunities and got into them while the getting was good.

While I may have experienced delays and detours during my journey, I was never lost. Two constants were always there to guide me: faith and intuition. I knew that God would provide what I needed to accomplish his goals for me. And I always trusted my gut instincts, even though they were sometimes wrong; I knew they were more often right.

Then one day I rounded a turn and realized, with no small measure of surprise, I had reached my young heart's desire. Every step taken, however contradictory it seemed, prepared me for what I had become. Every role filled, every person befriended, every good and bad decision, and every relationship formed propelled me to my appointed destination.

I discovered the truth behind the old wisdom that "no man is an island, complete unto himself." Without the others who came into my life, things would have turned out differently and probably not as well. Relationships are not only the key to business but also the key to life.

Today Miss Polly and her husband might be labeled mentors, or even life coaches. In simple, everyday terms, they were willing teachers to a willing student. The power of such willingness — on both sides — to make positive changes should never be underestimated. It has served me well.

Experience with these generous and caring business owners opened my eyes to the vital role relationships and team-building play in business, in success, and in life. It was the first time — but far from the last — that relationships and team-building proved their importance.

The Value of Learning

After several years, Miss Polly and her husband sold their business to an investment company. Because of the time, attention, and instruction they had given me, plus the expertise I had acquired, the president of the new company asked me to stay on as his assistant and run the office.

The student now had the opportunity to become a teacher; I was excited about the possibilities.

While assisting the new president in operations, I found it very fulfilling to teach others. Especially appealing was being in a position to implement new processes and identify ways to more effectively handle collections, payables, and other office details. As the company grew, it hired a certified public accountant.

Once again, I found a teacher willing to train me in a new set of skills. Studying these accounting practices also helped me learn firsthand the range of responsibilities of a CPA.

I loved numbers and was excited to work hard to learn everything about balance sheets and profit-and-loss statements. God had blessed me with a good brain, so I thanked Him by willingly and constantly using it.

As I continued to advance in the service industry division of the investment firm, my employer was prepping it for sale to a Fortune 500 company. I managed a staff for eight locations plus the centralized headquarters. In this role I learned to be a good manager as well as a leader. Our Vice President of Sales was a negotiations expert and another willing teacher of a new skill set.

After the sale, I became Controller and Regional Financial Manager for this new company. It was a corporate job — my first — with lots of responsibility, including thirteen offices in the U.S. and managing a staff of more than fifty. I submerged myself in it, loving every minute and growing in knowledge each day.

During this time my daughter Angela was born; I was now a working mom. I have never forgotten the difficulties of that stretch, which is why I work as creatively as possible to help other mothers juggle both of these responsibilities. It was the first time I felt I was somebody in the business world and I reveled in my new status — sometimes allowing the position to take priority over family interests and time.

This feeling of being important — of having power — can destroy if not held in check. When you have worked and dreamed about this status, you begin to think you deserve it. That power can turn you into a person you were not intended to be. There were times I did not treat my employees with the respect they deserved but instead treated them as if I owned their time. I made demands without considering their opinions or feelings.

In my personal life I was not able to balance my commitments as a mother, wife, and business executive and did not spend the time necessary to develop a family in the early years of marriage and motherhood. This is not the person I wanted to be, but the demands of the position I loved so much were great; I allowed my dream to take front seat for a while.

My marriage ended in divorce after seven years. I have to be honest and put some of the blame on me. I put my career ahead of my family, something I am not proud about. But I learned from it and did my best to make up for that with my daughter.

After some time, I began to see that I was not happy with the person I was becoming. Based upon my faith and values, I began to develop into the person I was intended to be. Part of this development was how I should treat each person in my life. To overcome the temptations of abusing a position of authority, each of us needs to have a secure value of who we are and how we will treat others. This is when the light came on; I was responsible for developing relationships with people in my life.

Directions Change

My whole world changed again when I met Charles Morgan. Like me, he had been married and divorced. He also had a daughter, and a son. These basic similarities drew us together, but the passion he had for business and leadership — plus his passion for people and life — were the real characteristics that proved to me I had at last found my soul mate.

Thirteen years after Miss Polly first offered me a job at the small service business, I left the company. This time, however, the move was dictated by my personal rather than business life. Although it seemed to be a defining step, it was instead just another transition. Shortly after Charles and I married, I took my second corporate job with another Fortune 500 company, a producer of steel products. There I learned many new skills, including converting financial records into foreign currency and setting up financials with one of the early personal computer programs.

I left that company after two years when Charles was selected to supervise the construction of an Alabama motor repair facility. Leaving my career behind and heading off to an unknown place was exciting but also scary. I was giving up my source of income with no guarantees I could step back into the corporate world at a later date. Knowing my daughter needed time with me and I needed time to blend our lives together with Charles' children made the decision the right one.

For a year-and-a-half I was a stay-at-home mom. Living in a small town and being away from business created the most stress-free time I had ever experienced, and I loved it — at least for a while.

But my mind still burned for business.

When Charles completed the project, we returned to Birmingham. I found work as a church financial manager, increasing my skills with computer programs and customer data. Setting up an electronic system that tracked donations by a unique number for each church member began my next level of data management.

To help make ends meet, I filled in with temporary weekend jobs. I was a mystery shopper and a movie theater auditor, to name a couple of my odd jobs. We struggled financially but worked hard to provide for the kids, and our marriage grew stronger through these times.

Charles was offered the position of Director of Engineering for an Atlanta-based long-term health care company operating more than eighty nursing homes and other facilities around the country. We moved again, and I found a project management job for a construction company that allowed me to work from home part of the time. Once again, teachers showed up and I learned project estimations and the development of proposals for customers as well as scheduling work and tracking progress and timelines. All those skills would come in handy years down the road.

Doors Open — Doors Close

After several years, professional changes paralleled our personal changes. Charles' employer announced plans to centralize operations, which would require we move to Arkansas.

Having finally realized his dream of moving to Atlanta, however, Charles wanted to stay put, so he bowed out of the company and established his own consulting and construction business, specializing in renovation work for nursing homes, hotels, and other commercial properties.

We developed partnership skills that later allowed us to be successful in starting MD&E. Charles had quite the entrepreneurial spirit and excelled at his business. After several years the economy rudely intervened with a downturn, and the stresses of paying bills and making payroll escalated. The strain took its toll; Charles had a heart attack and could no longer shoulder the combined burdens of the heavy workload and high anxiety.

As critical as Charles' business and income were, they were not worth the risks to his life. If we were to continue living in Atlanta, the answer was clear: I needed to provide for our family while Charles recovered, and I needed to do it quickly. Adding to the stress, we felt strongly we needed to repay our vendors on a large hotel project — the owner did not pay us.

As most people would probably do in that situation, I began by assessing my skills. I had an accounting background, as well as a variety of operational and business process experiences. I knew how to estimate a job in terms of personnel, materials, and hours. I knew how to write project plans and statements of work as well as proposals.

I had also worked with computers — the large mainframes and early personal computers — and had logged many hours on the trusty Radio Shack Tandy we bought when we moved to Atlanta. But my best skills were building relationships in the workplace, management, and critical thinking.

All this occurred around the time big corporations decided personal computers were the wave of the future. Companies began equipping employees with PCs and suddenly faced the daunting task of not only moving mountains of data from the mainframe to individual stations, but also customizing that data for specific positions and employees.

My computer experience and project management expertise helped me find a contract position with a major telecom company deploying PCs to its entire sales force. A dear friend of mine, a prayer partner at my church, knew the company she worked for was trying to form an IT division. She saw an opportunity for a contractor to come in, thought I could do it, and recommended me to management. Because the managers trusted her, they offered me the job. The door opened and I stepped through it. My job was to handle the transfer of data to those PCs.

Although I had computer experience, technology was not one of my natural talents. I stayed after hours to work through a multitude of issues to improve computer-based tasks. I took work home. I attended seminars. I logged countless hours learning new programs on my own.

I also developed valuable friendships with other employees. I met four strong, independent women who have since become my closest friends, always willing to be honest with me — and once again teachers entered my life. Like Miss Polly, they were willing to teach me; I was still willing to learn.

My strong management background allowed me to produce more efficient work than the other contractors on the project. Management soon asked me to take on an assistant and manage the other contractors.

I identified the problems with that situation right away, explained them to management, and presented a plan that would better serve the company's needs. I would hire, train, and manage people chosen by me. It wouldn't cost them any more than they were paying, and they wouldn't have the headaches of managing multiple contractors.

Well aware it could be the beginning or the end of my much-needed contract, as I made the proposal, I prayed.

Passion Drives Us

The company liked my solution and trusted me. That is how our new business was born.

I began by assuming use of the business my husband formed for his construction work, changed its focus to IT business solutions, and incorporated the company. I hired, trained, and managed the employees to my exacting standards of customer service, and coordinated the project to be sure my first customer received the best service.

Our newly formed company developed a system to meet the requirements of the business with data integration and customer information management. We tested the system rollout, provided user support, and developed reports and reporting systems.

Before long, we expanded to another large customer, supporting its service desk and deploying a customer relationship management tool. This project allowed me to see I needed more leaders to grow the company. It also helped me see that even as we grew, we should never forget to nurture our existing client relationships.

I continually taught myself about computers and data management, but was careful not to make the mistake of assuming that I was the only person capable of making good decisions for the company. I knew that to succeed, we would always need innovative ideas. I asked for, and often accepted, these ideas.

Some of my hires were straight out of college; my job was to help them grow — teach them what it takes to get along in the real world and how to conduct themselves in business. In return, they taught me more about computers, programming, and new processes. I took care of them and they supported me.

A successful business is not about "me" and "what I did." It's about what we can accomplish together.

Feeding the all-important "we" — strengthening relationships and building a team in the office — has always been my priority. From the days when Miss Polly first took me under her wing, I have believed training, nurturing, direction, and motivation of employees by management is the key to a successful business team. That is what makes a company fly or fall.

Don't fool yourself into thinking you can go it alone. Relationships change lives and guide businesses, and good relationships build happy lives and successful businesses.

Although I never got a college degree, I school myself in whatever I need to know to keep up with current business practices. I read constantly. I've gone through all of Stephen Covey's courses, and I'm a big fan of Dale Carnegie. I've also studied time management and other relevant subjects. I refuse to let myself fall behind the times.

I also believe in the value of good, old-fashioned common sense. You might feel intimidated when you're surrounded by the best and brightest at a conference table or in a boardroom.

But don't be intimidated.

Common sense can be a valuable ally in working through even the toughest issues. What people see as wisdom is often nothing more than simple common sense, and yours is as valid as anyone's.

The Price of Leadership

To stay ahead of the game is not easy. Often you must simultaneously manage and motivate employees, monitor and maximize work quality, promote and protect the business, satisfy old and attract new customers, anticipate and stay on top of trends and developments, and much more.

If you are like most business owners, this schedule helps keep you alive. The business is your passion and your heartbeat. For the first ten years of its existence, MD&E was my baby. It required all the work and worrying and wakeful nights such a relationship entails and had many of the same benefits. I worked along with my employees, side by side. Oftentimes during software releases we worked so hard and so late, it felt like I was constantly looking for anything to help us keep our focus during those long stretches. My desk was often loaded with Play Doh, marbles, yo-yos, and other toys, not to mention healthy snacks. Well, I did have some hidden chocolate for emergencies.

My complete devotion to the business was good and bad. Good because it taught my employees how much I cared about them and taught me how much they cared about me. It demonstrated that I was willing to get down and get dirty and do whatever they were doing, even if I wasn't as good at it as they were. But living through such closeness made it very difficult to let go of the daily work relationships.

As the company grew from its early level of twelve employees to its current level of more than eighty, it was necessary to acquire more HR knowledge. We gradually added benefits, starting with paid holidays and working up to the full package, including a 401(k) plan. It was a big step to cross the fifty-employee mark, the level at which the federal government requires small businesses to follow rules and regulations as stringent as those governing large corporations.

Letting go of managing all the details is a critically important lesson for business owners — and one I had trouble mastering. As the needs of the business changed, we began outsourcing our human resources work. With this move another teacher entered my life with lots of information and a different view, helping me master this change.

Sharing the Passion — Building Your Team

Some years ago I realized I did not want, nor could I afford, to continue working as long and hard as I had been. I made the decision to step away from day-to-day operations, turning them over to my staff so I could focus more on the big picture, forming a strategy to grow the company.

Owners are accustomed to being involved in every aspect of their company. Drawing back from the daily operation can be downright painful for both the owner and for the employees who have depended on the owner's decisions. My case was no different.

Turning loose a business — one in which you have shared all-nighters, birthed ideas, celebrated victories, and mourned losses — is painful. But that pain is a crucial step in the maturing of the company. You feel a long-suppressed freedom and take solace in knowing that your talented staff will grow to meet the company's needs when you stop holding their hands.

Turning loose also allowed me the opportunity to grow in my role as CEO and — together with my Board of Directors, which includes my husband — to plan the strategic direction of MD&E. This time has been filled with large challenges and many mistakes.

I found I could not move back and forth between strategic thinking and solving daily problems without underperforming at both. The best advice I can give you is this: Hire good, qualified managers; empower them to do their jobs; and don't micromanage.

Once I did that, I was able to focus on getting MD&E certified as a woman-owned business. We have used this certification as another avenue to grow. While going through the certification process is intense, doing so made me aware of gaps in our company structure. I wasted no time closing those gaps to have a healthier company. If I was stuck between strategy and daily operations, I may have missed or delayed this opportunity longer than would have been healthy for the business.

Schedule time to develop a strategic direction for yourself and your company. Once that direction is firm, make sure your entire team knows it so they can follow your lead. I find that getting out of the office with my executives in one- or two-day retreats allows us to better focus on developing and maintaining this strategy.

Peer groups are great for keeping you accountable to your focus and action plans. There are many of these groups available. One I highly recommend is Vistage, where we bring problems and discuss solutions plus accountability, something every good leader needs.

Letting go also allowed me to set aside true personal time vital to physical and emotional well-being. I had postponed this too often. But it didn't take long to reconnect to those lazy days of my youth when I had time to simply think and enjoy what I was doing without something screaming for my attention.

Business owners have a very real need to schedule time for themselves — and I don't mean a long lunch hour. Make it a date and don't break it.

Yes, you may envision the company falling apart without you there. It's only natural. But have confidence in the system. Your staff can handle things in your absence. If you surrounded yourself with people who show true leadership, the business will be fine. Your taking time off will do you — and them — a world of good.

Personal time relaxes and refreshes your mind and body, and helps you regain a fresh perspective that may have been dulled by too much time on the job. Most importantly, it allows you to get reacquainted with your family and/or reminds you that there is more to life than the business. Enjoy your personal time.

A more balanced life allows you to be a better leader.

I have gained much, both professionally and personally, by building a business with my husband. I've enjoyed financial benefits, of course, as well as the satisfaction of being my own boss and being able to follow our vision rather than someone else's.

Just as importantly, though, I have gained immense personal satisfaction, knowledge, strength, and many priceless relationships.

Family Dreams

There came a time when my husband and all three of our children, along with our daughter-in-law, worked at the business. Having them all was exciting, and our dreams for the future of the business involved them. When all three children chose to do something else, it hurt a little, which is only natural. Each discovered they had their own dreams to pursue and moved into an area that allowed them to have passion for what they are doing. My husband moved into a role on our Board of Directors and continues to offer advice and direction for our financial and marketing decisions.

I have to say it is now refreshing to get together as a family and not have the business be the center of conversation.

The rewards of owning a business have been great, but I also had to pay some rather steep prices in return. The biggest single sacrifice has been the loss of family time, which was especially difficult because I was not the only one who had to make that sacrifice. My devotion to the business was tough on a husband and child who were forced to do without the special attention that only a wife and mother can provide.

If I had it to do over, I would know my child and stepchildren's dreams better and help them to achieve them instead of assuming they would want to be a part of MD&E, which was our dream, not theirs. My husband and I looked at it as a way to provide for our children by having them work in the business instead of looking at the business as a way to provide for them to become the people they wanted to become.

Perhaps if we had created our business when the children were young, it would have been different, but each child felt they did not want to put the amount of time we did into running a business. Additionally, all had other ideas about how they would treat employees. Perhaps the experience I learned the hard way can't be understood unless you have felt them for yourself.

One lesson I would not repeat is having children report to me in a business situation. It is too much to balance personal and business. Personal is a part of who we are; you can't take that out of the situation, even in business. At the time, there were hurt feelings in the business setting, and these came home and had an impact on the family. Having a blended family did not help this situation as we had dynamics that created extra tension.

Watching and helping our children become successful in following their dreams has been very satisfying, though.

Legacy of Dreams

One thing I have noticed during years of beach visits is that no two sunsets are the same. Some evenings, the blazing sun slips instantly below the horizon. Not a trace remains of the light that shone brightly moments before. Other times, the radiance remains — hanging hazily over the horizon long after the sphere itself has dropped out of sight, the dim glow of red and orange reflecting on the water and clouds in a magical dance.

When I think of the future and the legacy I want to leave, that second sunset is the one I choose. I want the light of the people I helped — my family, the friends whose lives I have touched, and the impact of the work I have done — to continue to shine long after I have departed.

The legacy I want our company to leave is in its people and their relationships. It is in the passion for developing, maintaining, and loving those relationships through the good and the bad, the success and the failure. These are the true testimonials of our lives, for they are what make our lives worth living. The legacy of a person rests not in things but in the people whose lives have been enriched by their willingness to care.

Relationships are the foundation of business. Without them, a business cannot be successful.

Has it been worth it? I'm not sure I know the answer. And it is not a question I ask myself very often.

I do know that whatever I have done in and with my life defines who I am. If I made mistakes or took wrong turns, I can't undo them. I have to move on and make the best of what I am and what lies ahead.

For now, I look at my grandchildren and marvel at the love we share, knowing that this is how life should be. Life continues through those we love and what we pass on to the next generation.

I'm proud of my husband, my family, and my talented staff. I'm proud of what we were able to build with our own hands, vision, and hard work. There is no doubt in my mind that God blessed me by putting something out there He wants me to accomplish. I continue to reach for it, work for it, and sacrifice for it.

I am still working on being the best CEO possible for MD&E and have many new and exciting ideas for our future. I look forward to seeing where we can take MD&E, how our company will have a lasting legacy with the people and families who have benefited through relationships and faith.

We must plan for an orderly transition into the future. In doing that, we must train custodians for the future who will continue striving to touch lives in a positive way. I am proud of what I have accomplished with the powerful assistance of my faith and family and the strong, beneficial relationships along the way.

ORGANIZATIONS:

National Women Business Owners Corporation (certification: www.nwboc.org)

Greater Women's Business Council (certification: www.gwbc.biz)

Women's Business Enterprise National Council (certification: www.wbenc.org)

National Association of Women Business Owners (www.nawbo.org)

National Association of Professional & Executive Women (www.napew.com)

Atlanta Women in Business (www.atlantawomeninbusiness.com)

Technology Association of Georgia (www.TagOnline.org)

Vistage International (www.vistage.com)

Board Member, Dream House for Medically Fragile Children (www.DreamHouseForKids.org)

Tiffany Circle, Red Cross (www.RedCross.org)

Eleanor Morgan

MD&E, Inc. is a Certified Women-Owned Business that specializes in helping large organizations maximize the value of their CRM data. By organizing data, it helps customers streamline systems, increase revenues, and improve services.

Clarity Specialists/MD&E provides support for systems data management and consulting for major corporations. We have an 18-year track record of success in offering professional services in the Southeast.

MD&E, Inc.
3201 Peachtree Corners Circle • Norcross, Georgia 30092
(678) 291-9690 • emorgan@mdecorps.com
www.MDECorps.com • www.ClaritySpecialists.com

Chapter 5
Getting Started

I would like to start a business but am not sure exactly what to do. How can I identify my skill set and match it to a business type?

Eleanor: Will you be a technician or an entrepreneur? Either can create a successful business. Technicians provide a product customers are willing to pay for. Examples are writers, artists, and interior designers. The enterprise is dependent upon their skills, though, and when technicians don't contribute, their income dries up. Some technicians later decide to hire others to amplify their talent. That moves the technician into the realm of entrepreneur.

Entrepreneurs manage an enterprise that employs other people. Their skill set is to create strategy, manage, motivate, and build a profitable entity. After the development stage, the business can continue with or without their leadership.

My strongest skills were leadership and relationship-building, so my choice was to develop an enterprise.

For both technicians and entrepreneurs, creating a business takes innovation and marketing. Innovation is a hard, messy process. Mistakes will be made, but there are no shortcuts. The process creates wealth when successful.

Technicians seek customers willing to buy a product or service and trust it will be delivered. Entrepreneurs seek customers willing to trust their service or product when it has been produced by others.

Marketing isn't easy. In the real world, you don't have infinite resources or a perfect product or service, and you certainly don't sell to a growing market without competition.

Angela: Eleanor, that makes me a technician; I sell skills and knowledge and am not interested in having employees. However, I want to be the technician of choice with a team of vendors behind me that will maximize my ability to make money by offering a broader range of services and products. That is the best of both worlds.

To identify your skill set, first determine how you have made money. Do these skills lend themselves to other businesses? If so, you might have found a service to provide. Are you very good at something, and does research show there is a market for it? Get a piece of it. If there is no market, should there be? Make one and own it as a pioneer.

For instance, I loved to write and was good at it, but I wanted to make more money. I compared marketing materials used by businesses in my area to those representing national brands and asked: Can I offer my writing services to small, local companies at a lower rate and make them look good while I still make money? The answer was yes.

Peggy: You knew a market when you saw it, Angela. It's like the pioneer who created books on tape, or who recognized the needs of aging baby boomers and came up with the idea of day care for seniors. A landscaper came up with the idea of producing gardening DVDs.

Marla: Go in with a realistic understanding of the market and opportunities. Then match your interests with personal needs; this creates passion. I wanted to be able to use my management and marketing experience in a business I was interested in. I could relate to clients of medical spas. Owning one gave me a chance to investigate anti-aging treatments and use my selling skills. Finding my passion in life meant having more time to spend with family. Owning a business allowed me to work my schedule around personal needs because I wouldn't need to be physically on-site to effectively manage the business.

What is the most rewarding part of owning your own business?

Peggy: Start with personal growth, higher self-esteem, and not being afraid. For me, it is not about the money, although money is a great motivator.

Eleanor: Knowing I am creating my legacy with an ongoing system support business, MD&E, that will be able to provide for employees and their families with or without my direct involvement. My faith, dreams, and passion gave me opportunities to help others get where they wanted in their own lives. I like supporting my church, community, and other nonprofit organizations financially through blessings I have received.

Marla: My focus on life and priorities is clearer now that I am out of Corporate America and have taken control of my future. My proactive approach added balance in my family life, which ultimately brings me more happiness.

Angela: More than anything I have enjoyed learning about my customers' businesses. I could not have learned these things as an employee. It has allowed me to try on other careers and industry types to see if I would like them should I ever get tired of what I do.

What questions should I ask myself before I start a business?

Peggy: Is this just a fleeting fantasy or am I committed for the long haul?

Marla: Will I have enough cash flow? Am I willing to make adjustments to my lifestyle if money runs low?

Eleanor: Do I have a double dose of energy? Deep passion? Good health? Fun relationships personally as well as in business? Have I planned thoroughly and raised a year's worth of funding?

Angela: Do I fail well? Starting out, business owners fail more than they succeed. The learning curve can be steep. If you fail, identify what you learned, improve your process, and move on to success. The learning curve will not be as steep in my next business because I will follow these lessons. Failure is not permanent. Staying in the I-am-a-failure state of mind is a problem.

What is the number one mistake you made when you started your business?

Angela: I did not invest in myself and turned down opportunities to learn about the writing industry if I had to pay. Had I done so, I would have made more money more quickly. I did not see the benefits of investing in education; I isolated myself far too long.

Marla: Getting bad advice from a consultant. Unrealistic expectations built into the business plan impeded cash flow and slowed progress. Startup costs and requirements for working capital were significantly affected.

Peggy: Not having a business plan, goals, or strategies. The launch of my image consulting business would have gone smoother with specific goals (such as five clients in the first six months or $60,000 in revenue the first year) and a business plan with strategies I could measure.

Eleanor: Underestimating the value of my leadership to the success of the company. As I built MD&E, I needed to have the final word on hiring, firing, training, working with the customer, creating sales, making proposals, maintaining a positive cash flow, and marketing. I also had to motivate and develop a strong support team. I needed to keep non-seasoned employees focused on the strategic plan. I needed for customers to trust the team I was building.

When I started out, I had no idea how much leadership and focus would be necessary or how much growing a company would take from my personal life and finances. Successful leaders have to be willing to put business needs first when necessary. There were times I didn't make birthday celebrations or take classes or just hang out with my children or spouse. When you are the owner, there are times you can't delegate a time-sensitive problem. Remember, this is your baby.

Be prepared to use personal funds to finance areas of your business. Many times, my husband and I borrowed to meet payroll long before we were paid by the customer. You have to believe in your business and its capacity to repay these loans.

What do I need to make a business happen?

Marla: Determination, a self-motivated attitude, and a good support network.

Peggy: Passion, passion, passion! If you are not addicted to what you do, you shouldn't even start. If passion is missing, chances for success are nil.

Eleanor: A willingness to learn from mistakes. You won't have the time or money to make the same mistakes twice, so learn quickly. However, don't hesitate too long over decisions. Have faith in your abilities and roll with the punches. Soak up positive energy from family and friends; you will need it.

Angela: Sometimes it takes a willingness to look like a fool as you try things you have never done or follow a path others may not understand. Don't be afraid to fail.

What helped you the most when you started your business?

Peggy: The support of my husband and friends, and money in the bank that allowed me to spend the first six months developing my business without needing an income from it.

Marla: Faith in myself and the plan God intended for me. I am thankful I had the fortitude to understand, accept, and seize the opportunities put in front of me. I was able to leave a comfortable job and create a happier life for my family and myself.

Eleanor: I had faith in God's direction for me. Business and personal relationships supported my passion; the main energy came from me. It was based on an internal voice that told me this was the right thing to do.

Angela: Exactly, Eleanor. When I tried to convince my internal voice it was wrong, it kept hounding me. Sometimes you choose when to start a business; sometimes circumstances choose you. The way I did it (office in the home, hardly any overhead, some profit shown almost immediately) provided a needed boost to my ego. Customers were happy with what I did, and I was earning money from my own efforts. I was able to focus on something positive and constructive.

I am thinking about hiring a consulting firm. How do I know I am getting what I need and not wasting money?

Marla: Consultants can be valuable if you understand how to use them. Their worth is based on depth of experience in your industry or market.

Assess the packages offered and be open to advice and evaluations. Business owners, typically Type-A personalities, like to take control by being involved in every decision. This approach could slow the progress of the business if the owner passes up a good solution because it involves risk or cost. Business owners must be careful not to allow personal pride to prevent them from listening to good advice. Keep an open mind when dealing with consultants, but be perceptive enough to know when they aren't delivering good answers for your unique business.

Peggy: Marla, I wish I had known you when I started my company. I hired consultants left and right. I had coaches, mentors, advisers, and more, yet never took time to apply what I learned. I was on to the next project. When working with a coach, space out the sessions to give yourself time not only to digest what you have learned, but to put it into practice.

Eleanor: Be sure to interview carefully and match the consulting firm's style and budget to your organization. Consultants can bring a variety of talents and expertise to an organization that can't afford it up front. Have them set up processes you will be able to maintain. Ask for advice in areas outside your expertise.

My company is just me. Do I need a mission statement? If so, what should be in it?

Marla: Formal and informal mission statements clearly define a goal for both your business and your customers. When written, a mission statement helps hold everyone accountable for the service you want to provide customers, shareholders, employees, and yourself.

Peggy: A mission statement can be a set of values you were taught or ones you choose for yourself as an adult. It could be as simple as The Golden Rule: "Treat others as you want to be treated."

Eleanor: A mission statement expresses the purpose of your business and puts everyone on the same page. Constructed properly, it lends direction and establishes measurements of success. In addition, a company could have a vision statement (expressing strategic direction) and a statement of core values (beliefs and ethics that comprise your business culture).

Angela: My mission statement is informal. I want to treat my customers so well they will stay loyal to me through thick and thin. Plus, I want them to trust I always have their best interests at heart. I want them to know I will never lie to them to make a buck. From that foundation all other customer relations and business decisions flow.

Chapter 6
Needs & Support

How can I identify my personal needs?

Marla: My personal needs are defined by core ethics and determining what is important to me. Personal and professional needs must be aligned if you want to achieve happiness.

Angela: I wasn't happy and didn't know why. I examined each decision I made, asked why I made it, and looked at the outcome. If the outcome was beneficial to me and my family, I stayed with it. If it wasn't, I changed course. Eventually I got a feel for what I needed.

Eleanor: Personal needs feed you internally, creating stamina and passion. I was driven by the desire to create something that allows me to give back to others. Positive relationships are keys to fulfilling personal needs.

Peggy: I was happy in the corporate world. But, after being laid off for the fifth time, I wondered whether I should try something else. My husband was planning to retire in a few years, my mother would be spending more time in the U.S., and I felt I needed more flexibility in my life. We also wanted to purchase a second home. If I worked for someone else, I'd be able to go there only two weeks a year. That made no sense.

How can I identify my professional needs?

Marla: Start by considering a few questions. Why are you starting a business? Are you seeking power? Do you simply want to make a living? Are you looking for more opportunity to use your intelligence? Do you want to have more flexibility to be creative? Are others pushing you to do what they want? What are your talents? What interests you most? What are your strengths?

Peggy: What benefits do you want in life? What kind of business would give you those?

Angela: After assessing the big picture, keep going. Can you do what it takes to improve your skills? What will happen if you don't improve your skills? Finally, climb onto the psychiatrist's couch. Are you actually afraid of success? If so, why?

Eleanor: I speak for all when I say it is crucial to think about what you are willing to give back to a profession in addition to what you hope to receive. By doing so, you can identify support and learning opportunities important to long-term happiness and stability. Some of the questions brought up here will be difficult to answer — but they played a vital role in our lives. Again, what drives your passion?

How can I determine whether my personal and professional needs will work together?

Marla: Again, be honest with yourself. Do I act by one set of standards at work that are the opposite of my personal values? Am I unhappy because of that?

Peggy: Will my immediate family give me support while I start my business? Will they understand when I must take some time away from them to network? Do they know they may need to tighten their belts until the business starts to make a profit?

Angela: Will my family be harmed emotionally or financially when I start this business?

Eleanor: If, after these calculations, you decide to start a business, never neglect personal needs. They subconsciously influence whether you feel the business is successful. For example, if you are not willing to wait to build a company, look for a business in which you are the technician or directly control your destiny. Balancing personal and professional needs makes it easier to get up the next morning after a bad day.

When I get in the real world, I become paralyzed with fear and doubt my abilities and knowledge. What can I do to overcome this fear?

Peggy: Practice, practice, practice. Don't wing it. If you know your business, you can be confident in selling the benefits of it to customers. Prepare, prepare, prepare before you do anything. With practice and preparation your confidence will grow.

Angela: Some people must overcome always believing the worst about themselves. Peggy is right about practice and preparation. In every field, top performers prepare for what they are not good at. Talented amateurs practice what they are good at and may identify shortcomings, but do not work on them with gusto. Those satisfied with the status quo never identify an opportunity for improvement, much less work on it. Therefore, if you have mapped a plan and are working on it, you are by definition a high performer. Congratulations. You will be fine; the fear and doubt lessens over time.

How important is support from outside the family?

Eleanor: It is essential. Everyone has to have support — physical, emotional, and spiritual.

Angela: I was so focused on family needs that at first I labored with no support whatsoever. My family saw my writing business as something that would never interfere with their schedules or needs. I admit their attitude was my doing. At first I didn't have many customers, but as more came aboard and needed me on the occasional weekend, evening, or early morning, the family had to understand.

Because I was in uncharted waters, I needed to talk to other women who had been there and had practical advice to offer. The more we talk to other women who have been there and done that, the quicker we can balance our professional and personal lives.

Marla: Support outside the family helps keep your decisions unbiased. This is especially important if the business owner has financial concerns that could dramatically affect decisions about the company, hampering its ability to move forward. If you do not explore opinions beyond your immediate feedback group, you risk making decisions based upon silos of information.

This is why corporations put outsiders on their boards of directors. It allows an external influence to assess the direction of the company and avoids some of the biases associated with people on the payroll.

Where can I get support from outside the family?

Peggy: Friends, colleagues, business associations, local colleges and universities; it's there for the asking.

Eleanor: Almost all professional organizations have local chapters. Each is different, based on the personality and style of the members. Attend as many as you can to determine the group best suited for you. Look for peers who will give and take advice and hold you accountable for decisions. The organization from which I have received the most support and direction is Vistage. I meet with peers for a full day each month and have a monthly session with the chairperson. The National Association of Women Business Owners has a great CEO Roundtable series. Lots of other organizations offer small group settings.

Angela: It may take a year or two to find the group that best supports your personal and business needs. In Atlanta my first support network was the locally focused Atlanta Women in Business. I was able to move forward with my business because I had benchmarks against which to measure myself. I could see what I did and did not want to do, based upon what others in the group had done and how it turned out.

This affiliation also gave me the confidence to move out nationally into other groups. I served as president of the Atlanta chapter of the National Association of Professional Women and became a member of the National Association of Women Business Owners.

Eleanor: A support network also brings balance in life. Too many of us treat association memberships as an afterthought. We seek out people who can advance our careers but not enrich them. It is a sad commentary on overscheduled, overstuffed modern lifestyles that we need practical reasons to interact with people. Too many educated, personable professionals must be taught how to meet and bond with fellow humans. The simple act of human connection should be the most natural thing in the world, but it has become something of a lost art — a relic we must leave behind to maintain the frantic pace of our lives.

I have no clue what the market is paying for the types of services or products I want to offer. How do I decide how to price them?

Peggy: Check with competitors and people who have similar businesses. Ask friends and relatives what they have paid for the product or service you provide. Or hire a research firm to perform a competitive analysis.

Marla: Before you set a price, understand the costs involved to perform the service or produce the product. Once a tentative price is set, compare it to the competition. If your price is lower, move it closer to the competition. You'll make more money and avoid sending the wrong message — that you are the substandard alternative.

Of course, you may intend to be the lower-cost alternative. However, I still recommend not creating a big gap in price until you have established a brand and a track record. If your price is much higher than the competition's, you must control costs better. If you are intentionally setting your price higher to attract a more exclusive market, be sure you have a product or service that will match expectations.

Suppose potential competitors are unwilling to share pricing information? Where can I get it?

Marla: Most business owners are willing to help. Talking with them may open doors of opportunity for buyouts, partnerships, etc. Industry consultants often have this sort of information. Testing competitors from a customer's perspective helped me realize there was a great need for good customer service and follow-up in medical spas.

Peggy: I was astonished to find that seasoned image consultants were willing to give me the dirt on having my own image consultancy. Of course, I was not competition to them at the time, but all the people I asked were very generous with tips and advice.

Angela: I could not get anyone locally in the writing and graphic design businesses to share, so I called similar businesses outside my market. Also, a local printer I used for a customer's projects gave me a lot of good advice about pricing strategies. She was willing to share because she was a vendor for me and not competition.

I am not sure whether I should have my customers or clients sign a contract for my services. When are contracts necessary?

Eleanor: Nearly everything you do for customers needs to be documented. Contracts are an extension of that. Depending on the complexity and depth of services or products offered, contracts might need to be developed or reviewed by a lawyer. In my industry, systems data support, we deal with proprietary processes, so contract language is critical. Make sure each party understands the services and price, the billing procedure, and when payment is expected, among other things.

Marla: In the health care field, we have contracts, consents, understanding of consents, policies and procedures — all to protect us from lawsuits. If customers refuse to sign, they cannot purchase services. Privacy is a big issue in health care, and I must make sure I am doing everything possible to maintain a client's privacy. Also, if contract language can be interpreted in different ways, the contract is useless. That can hurt you.

Peggy: If not a formal contract, at least have a signed letter of understanding or an outline you and the client both sign. One of my colleagues in image consulting had a client ask for her money back after a color analysis. The client said her sister did not agree with the colors recommended. Another colleague said her client did not want to pay for several hours of personal shopping because no appropriate clothes were found. (I personally believe these demands came from con artists, and there are a lot of them out there.)

When you are in a service industry and get paid for your time, you need to protect yourself. Time is an intangible, and some clients don't see the value of it. A contract helps you and the client understand the goals and objectives up front. Having a written agreement gives you more leverage to get paid.

Angela: As a writer, I don't have these issues. My contracts consist of e-mailed quotes followed by acceptances and sign-offs by e-mail. I print out and save all correspondence.

What are startup costs? How can I determine what mine will be?

Eleanor: Startup costs for an entrepreneur may include incorporation fees, market surveys, advertising, rent, equipment, salaries (including yours), and possible travel expenses. This is spent before you have a paying customer. Tax regulations require some costs to be amortized over a period of time as opposed to being expensed during the month they occurred; check with your CPA. Our original startup costs at MD&E included a fee for incorporating, a business license, a minimum outlay for equipment, and my salary.

Angela: It depends. My hard startup costs consisted of business cards, a business license, gas for my car, a Day Timer calendar, and a word processor. My office was in my home. It all probably ran around $800.

Peggy: I took over my husband's home office, which he was no longer using. Use a space separate from the living area; working on the dining room table will not be productive. My startup costs were education, training, coaching, a separate phone line, a Web site, the services of a CPA, and a lawyer to set up my company's structure. I spent $20,000.

Marla: My startup costs were significant because of building codes dictated for the medical spa industry. As a new company, I had to assess my position in relation to the competition and determine what I needed to differentiate myself. There were closing fees, loan fees, inventory, Web design, logo design, printing, equipment, training, and advertising. Hard costs (lease, telephone, etc.) don't change. Soft costs (advertising, cleaning services, etc.) can vary.

It is important that you understand how much money is needed to begin and maintain your business. In my case, I underestimated how much I would need because I relied too heavily on projections from a consultant. I also got hit with a recession. My husband became a guarantor for my loans so I could refinance and free up capital.

When you start a business, you should have enough cash flow to allow for extraordinary circumstances that could occur outside the business plan.

What big financial mistakes do business owners often make?

Peggy: Doing everything pro bono because you need the experience. It's hard to charge what you are worth when your only work experience has been getting paid by a company that determined what your services were worth.

Angela: Undercharging to get your foot in the door and then never raising prices to accurately meet the local market. Plan for surprise costs. You think you know everything that goes into the business, only to be shocked when costs come in double what you planned.

Marla: Not making sure you are getting the best price from vendors. Look for creative ways to save. I paid an employee to clean the spa. That helped her make more money, and because she was an employee, she did a better job than an outside company. I also began bartering for advertising, printing services, carpentry work, and window cleaning.

Eleanor: Trying to do everything on your own and setting unrealistic financial projections. Have a business plan. Seek relevant advice. Define your customer and keep an eye on competitors.

Wow. That's a lot of mistakes. How can I avoid them?

Peggy: Do a lot of research and network with people who have similar businesses.

Eleanor: Identify other organizations successful in the business segment you are targeting. Find out how they are structured and identify what they do best. Research from outside firms can be costly. Look for other ways to get the information.

Marla: You will make mistakes. Learning from them is how you grow. By reading this book you have already taken the necessary step of learning from the mistakes of others. Never stop exploring options in your field or market. It is vital to be open to opportunity and change.

Angela: Be realistic. Get the stars out of your eyes. Run the numbers and confirm you have accurate numbers to begin with. Don't get sentimental about your services and products. If something is not working, change it.

What is a business plan?

Eleanor: It's a roadmap that describes the business, the marketing plan, the competition, operating procedures, and personnel requirements. Financial data are quantified by spelling out initial capital and loan requirements, projected revenue and expenses, and projected cash flow.

A business plan develops into a financial budget that compares actual sales and costs with projected sales and costs. As your business matures, you compare current-year revenues and costs to the same period the previous year and see if you need to adjust expenses.

The document itself typically starts with an executive summary and then details the target market and operating plan. Financial data must have supporting documentation. Then there's the roadmap: You know you are going to point B from point A, but there are various ways to do that. Spell out how you will adjust for economic conditions. If you don't know where you are going, you will never get there.

Breaking down a business plan by sections:

- **Executive summary:** A high-level overview defining your business and a projection of how much time and capital will be needed for it to become profitable.

- **Marketing summary:** Identifies the target market and what efforts will be necessary to reach it. A key ingredient is a projection of the number and type of sales professionals necessary.

- **Operating plan:** Defines the processes necessary to produce the product or service. If you need other team members, this is where you spell out how much they will cost.

- **Financial data:** Expected sales and the costs to produce them. How much money will you need to get the product or service ready to generate revenue?

- **Supporting documents:** The market analysis and budget assumptions.

Eleanor/Peggy: After the business plan has been developed, the process moves along:

Step 1: Develop a three- to five-year projection of income and expenses. Plan how much cash will be needed for operations. Invest in accounting resources appropriate for the size of the company.

Step 2: Develop a detailed budget for the current year.

Step 3: Break down expenses into individual items that can be compared monthly or quarterly. Those comparisons will eventually be made year-over-year — that is, apples-to-apples comparisons with the same period the year before.

Step 4: Determine which items cost more than expected. Correct overruns and keep profit margins to sustain a successful operation.

Sounds complicated. Do I need a business plan?

Eleanor: Yes, if you plan to seek outside financial assistance.

Marla: It expresses your financial vision for the company. Putting a business plan together is a great way to spend money on paper. It lets you try out various business types, product mixes, and other possible market opportunities before you spend a dime. You may find your idea will not work when you run the numbers.

Once you start a business, the plan can be used to get a picture of future cash flow. If you lease a facility in a highly visible, upscale location, potential landlords may request a copy of the business plan, too; they want to ensure you have a plan for success before they agree to do business with you.

Comparing financial results against the business plan sounds great, but can you define and simplify how it is done?

Peggy: Start by budgeting, so you know how much money must come in weekly or monthly to turn a profit. When necessary, lower expenses. If revenue is less than expected, analyze it. Does your business have seasonal fluctuations? Are you focusing on the wrong markets? Are you undercharging? Did the competition attract or keep customers by lowering its rates to meet or beat yours?

Then it may be time for tougher questions: Can you identify another market to bring in more revenue? Can you raise rates? Can you find a weakness in the competition's offerings and use that as a marketing tool?

I have a business but would like to make more profit. How can I identify opportunities that will move me into a more profitable phase?

Angela: Existing customers are already loyal and trust you. In what other ways can you help them? Expand product offerings? Expand services? Become a knowledgeable source for them on other matters? It costs less to keep and service an existing customer than to find a new one.

Peggy: That's true. Current customers are the best future customers; give them the opportunity to buy more. Stay in touch with clients and make sure they know all the services you provide and how these services can have a positive impact on them. But be a specialist, not a generalist. Work on finding your niche or else you will be nothing to everyone and everything to no one.

Marla: Take another look at your cost plan to see if there are areas where you can save. For instance, in my medical spa business we were initially open seven days a week. When I analyzed staffing costs against revenue, I saw the need to close on Sundays and Mondays. This made the other days more profitable.

Research trends in your industry. I had to enter the liposuction segment, even though I had no intention to do so. In my market, this eventually became the service that generated the highest revenue. I either had to enter the market or allow my service menu to be cannibalized by other providers that offered better overall results for a similar price.

What is the value of cash flow?

Peggy: A positive cash flow — more money coming in than going out — is the engine that makes a business hum. It provides you the freedom to take risks, reach out to new markets, and turn down opportunities that may not be the best fit. Had you needed the money, you might have had to accept those jobs.

Cash flow lets you sleep peacefully because you don't have to work with someone with whom you have no chemistry. One of the perks of being self-employed is picking and choosing the people I work with. Less stress, more peace of mind. I want my business to be a win/win. I want to help my clients but also want the experience to be rewarding for me. If I work with someone just for the money, it's not worth the aggravation.

Eleanor: In a larger company such as MD&E, tracking cash flow is critical for planning purchases and making payroll. We have a large payroll that we pay every other week, but our customer payments are not received until 60 or 90 days later. Having a positive cash flow is like keeping enough in your checking account to cover the credit card bill before the next paycheck arrives.

How can I identify factors that derail accurate financial planning?

Angela: It is amazing how many people start a business and their only planning is high hopes. They assume everybody will want what they have to sell, but they wake up a few months later in debt, out of business, and wondering what went wrong.

Know your competition. If you think no one else is doing what you do, you're wrong. It's depressing to call on a potential customer and hear "ABC Company already does that for me; you know them, right? They are great."

Eleanor: Larger enterprises should test all financial assumptions against the results of other organizations that have been through what you are attempting. Another possibility is outside research, if the firm understands your industry.

I would like my company to become certified as a woman-owned business. What are the pros and cons of becoming certified?

Eleanor: Becoming a certified woman-owned business requires an in-depth review of your organization. That includes, if applicable, stock ownership, company minutes, the hierarchy of the organization, company and personal financial information, whether or not you are a Sub S or LLC company, and more. If you are not going use the certification to attract contracts, this can be a costly investment. Certification is not a networking opportunity. However, if you work with customers who have diversification programs, or if you want to bid for state, local, or federal contracts, certification is a must and well worth the investment.

Marla: For more information, contact the National Association of Women Business Owners (www.nawbo.org) or the Women's Business Enterprise National Council (www.wbenc.org).

Peggy: I was advised to be certified, but I didn't see the value. Most of my business comes from referrals.

Angela: I, too, was advised to become certified, with the promise of huge rewards. But in my opinion as a sole proprietor, certification programs promise more than they deliver. I think that point should be made clearer in marketing efforts. I did become WBENC-certified, but no matter how I worked in the system, I never could get an opportunity to be either a first, second, or third tier provider and make a profit while doing so. The work involved for the payoff was not worth it.

Do I need a Certified Public Accountant (CPA)?

Eleanor: A CPA can assist by identifying licenses, types of insurance, and tax registration necessary. You can hire a CPA, use an outside firm or accounting service, or do the tasks yourself.

As a startup grows, a CPA can provide other services, such as:

- Designing and installing systems that track costs as well as profit and loss.

- Securing and restructuring financing as well as developing banking relationships, including producing the documents necessary to secure loans and shopping for the lowest interest rate.

- Developing cash flow models. You need to know when you will have cash for major investments or to take a dividend out of your business.

- Identifying ways to improve profitability by looking at each expense, such as the cost of insurance and workers' compensation.

- Advising on potential mergers, acquisitions, and divestitures when appropriate.

- Designing and implementing employee compensation and benefit packages. These plans help you attract and keep the best talent.

- Ensuring compliance with government regulations. Examples: sales tax compliance, estimated payroll taxes, year-end taxes, and workers' comp audits.

Peggy: Of course you need a CPA. Spend your time where you make money. Unless you are a CPA, don't waste time with bookkeeping.

Marla: But take into account the level of your financial skills and the size of your company. It can be costly to use accounting services. This is not one of my strengths, so it was a necessary cost. What matters is that the process is done properly.

Angela: My business is not incorporated and therefore does not have to meet complicated legal codes. My bookkeeping requirements are manageable, so I do not need an outside accountant, certified or not.

Should I incorporate?

Eleanor: A proprietor typically incorporates to establish a legal separation between the business entity and her personal assets. Under certain circumstances, establishing a business provides tax advantages.

Marla: Consult your CPA or financial adviser. The situation is different for everyone. Sometimes a Limited Liability Company (LLC) is more effective, based upon the ownership ratio of the business. Your classification will determine your personal liability in the event of a disaster or bankruptcy.

Peggy: Even a small company should separate personal assets from business assets. You never know what could happen. Consult an attorney or accountant to select the best legal structure.

Angela: I have not incorporated for several reasons. One: the added paperwork and costs. Two: As a writer, I am not performing services that in any way, shape, or form could cause death or injury, so my worry about being sued is greatly lessened. Three: If I incorporate, how I pay myself becomes more complicated, and I don't want that complication.

I have decided to incorporate. What structure would be best?

Eleanor: This is where you definitely bring in a lawyer and a CPA. Here's a memo from my CPA, Reno Borgognoni. He stresses that these are guidelines and are no substitute for hands-on professional advice appropriate to your situation:

First, weigh all factors such as type of business, the product or service offered, your individual financial and income tax situation, whether other family or non-family partners or co-owners will be involved, financing needs, and succession plans.

Other than the full corporate legal entity (the C Corporation), entities to consider are the General Partnership, the Limited Liability Partnership (Ltd.), the Limited Liability Company (LLC), and the Subchapter S Corporation.

Key questions to consider:

Liability: LLCs and corporations shield personal assets. Would your business benefit from the limited liability afforded by incorporating?

Costs and fees: These include incorporation fees, annual franchise fees (if applicable), creation of an accounting system, and the maintenance of corporate bank accounts. Would the disadvantage of incorporating exceed the benefits?

Complexity: Maintaining a corporate structure, implementing proper accounting systems and procedures, conducting annual meetings, and filing annual reports with the state imposes a huge time commitment. Would meeting these requirements hinder your business?

Taxation issues: Would the tax burden on you and your business decrease, increase, or remain unchanged? Would you benefit from the pass-through taxation of an S Corporation or through paying corporate taxes as a C Corporation?

Fringe-benefit packages: Would you benefit from the tax deductibility of the fringe-benefit package offered to shareholder employees, enjoyed by C Corporations, as opposed to having those fringe benefits taxed as income to the employee, as is required of S Corporations?

Investors and employees: Would the greater flexibility offered through the issuance of stock, and the possibility of offering stock options, help attract investors as well as attract and retain key employees?

Structure: Would your business benefit from the structure required of corporations, with the various rights and duties of corporate stockholders, directors, and officers?

Succession planning: Would the fact that the corporate structure continues indefinitely, with transfer of ownership possible through the sale or transfer of stock, assist with succession planning or estate planning?

Transfer of shares: Would your business benefit from the ability to transfer shares? Could you adequately control any risk of shares being transferred to or inherited by undesirable parties by implementing a buy-sell agreement restricting the transfer of stock?

Regulatory filings: Would you be required to disclose information into public records, such as the identity of your corporation's directors, that you would prefer remain confidential?

Corporation or LLC: Many businesses receive adequate protections from liability by forming as a Limited Liability Company while avoiding much of the cost and complexity of forming as a C Corporation. Discuss this choice with your lawyer and CPA.

Advantages of Incorporation

Limited liability: The sole proprietor assumes all liabilities of the company. Personal assets, such as your house and car, can be seized to pay the debts of your business. When a business incorporates, an individual shareholder's liability is limited to the amount she invested in the company; you can't be held responsible for the debts of the corporation unless you've given a personal guarantee.

Corporations carry on: A corporation has an unlimited life span and will continue to exist even if the shareholders die or leave the business, or if the ownership changes.

Raising money is easier: The ability of corporations to raise money may make it easier for the business to grow and develop. Corporations can borrow and incur debt; they can also sell shares of stock to raise equity capital.

Income control: If you incorporate your small business, you can determine when you personally receive income and whether the income is earned income or dividend income, a real tax advantage.

Potential tax deferral: Incorporation allows you to defer paying some taxes. Thus, you may be able to realize tax savings if you move to a lower tax bracket, or if tax rates have fallen.

Income splitting: Another tax advantage of incorporating. Corporations pay dividends to their shareholders from the company's earnings. A shareholder does not have to be actively involved in business activities to receive dividends. Your spouse and/or children could be shareholders, giving you the opportunity to redistribute income from family members in higher tax brackets to family members with incomes that are taxed at a lower rate.

Cachet: Having Ltd., Inc., LLC, or Corp. as part of your company's official name may increase business because people perceive corporations as being more stable than unincorporated businesses. If you're a contractor, you may also find that some companies will do business only with incorporated companies because of liability issues.

Disadvantages of Incorporation

Another tax return: When you incorporate your small business, each year you'll have to file taxes personally and for the corporation. This, of course, means more accounting fees.

More filings: There is a lot more paperwork involved in maintaining a corporation than a sole proprietorship or partnership. Corporations, for example, must maintain minutes from corporate meetings. Other corporate documents, which must be kept up to date, include the register of directors, the share register, and the transfer register. Penalties for neglect can be severe.

No personal tax credits: Being incorporated may actually be a tax disadvantage for certain businesses. Corporations are not eligible for personal tax credits. Every dollar a corporation earns is taxed. As a sole proprietor, you may be able to claim tax credits a corporation could not.

Losses are handled differently: A corporation doesn't have the same flexibility in handling business losses as a sole proprietorship or a partnership. As a sole proprietor, if your business experiences operating losses, you can use them to reduce other types of personal income in the year the losses occur. Unless certain tax-advantaged elections are made, a corporation's losses can only be carried forward or back to reduce income from other years.

Liability may not be as limited as you think: Limiting liability is the prime advantage of incorporating, but that may be undercut by personal guarantees and/or credit agreements. The corporation's much-vaunted limited liability is irrelevant when no lender will give the corporation credit. When a corporation has what lending institutions consider insufficient assets to secure a loan, lenders often insist on personal guarantees from the business owner(s). So although technically the corporation has limited liability, the owner still ends up being personally liable if the corporation can't meet its repayment obligations.

Registering is expensive: Corporations are more expensive to set up. A corporation is a more complex legal structure than a sole proprietorship or partnership, so it's logical that creating one would be more complicated.

Eleanor: Reno has covered the legalities. Time for some reality: Whether to incorporate shouldn't be an entrepreneur's first decision. Go build your business. As soon as the income, expenses, and operating methods become clear, you'll be able to explain your model to lawyers and CPAs. They'll provide you the input necessary to help with the next step — determining what filings would be appropriate and setting up an accounting system.

Chapter 9

Peggy on Branding
Branding Q&A

The Importance of Branding

By Peggy M. Parks, AICI CIP

In her book *Make a Name for Yourself: Eight Steps Every Woman Needs to Create a Personal Brand Strategy for Success*, Robin Fisher Roffer makes it clear from the get-go that "if you do not brand yourself, someone else will!"

But what exactly is branding?

Atlanta Women in Business Founder and Principal Lya Sorano defines it as "an image associated with a name." What do you think of when you hear Nike or Rolex? What image pops into your mind when offered a Coke?

A brand is a calling card. It's who you are, what you do, how you do it, and how potential clients can identify and distinguish your services from the rest of the pack.

How you brand yourself can mean the difference between success and failure, especially for a startup.

The Small Business Administration reports that 50% to 75% of new businesses fail because they don't establish an identity with customers. In the fiercely competitive world in which we live — and buy — branding has become absolutely fundamental in terms of putting your product or service out there and making it sell.

Successful corporations understand this. They spend millions of dollars developing, supporting, and maintaining their brands. Why? Because branding not only helps customers identify products and services they like, it also induces them to buy.

Examples of excellent branding abound. For instance, mention Rachael Ray and your mind immediately leaps to 30-minute meals. Through her television program, magazine, cookbooks, and her bubbly persona, Ray has created a brand consumers identify with quick, stress-free cooking.

For smaller businesses, branding is no less significant. Entrepreneurs must develop and maintain a distinctive brand identity — it's critical to their success. I have seen the need for branding on a personal level in my work as an Atlanta-based image consultant. To attract and maintain an elite clientele, it is vital that I cultivate a professional, courteous, well-groomed, and worldly reputation. Workshops, monthly newsletters, and an informative blog also help me brand my company and establish expertise in the image and etiquette industry.

Determine Your Message

Let's say you're an entrepreneur who has decided to open a clothing boutique or set up a catering service.

A crucial part of getting a business started is to step back and think about what makes your company original and unique. What sort of reputation would you like to have? What can customers expect from you that they can't get from your competitors? Do you have a particular style or area of expertise that sets you apart? The answers will guide the establishment of your brand and the message you deliver to the public.

Will your boutique be stocked with only local, up-and-coming designers? This is a unique facet that, if branded successfully, can help you appeal to the "localvore" community as well as tourists looking for something special. Will your catering business provide a gourmet, epicurean experience, targeting a high-end clientele, or the comforting taste of Mom's home cooking?

Your brand needs to clearly convey your particular niche, so people know what to expect.

Branding Tools and Techniques

Once you've nailed down your branding message, it's time to implement methods that reinforce that message.

Remember: Be consistent. Part of developing a successful personal brand is ensuring that all components of your business send the same message to customers and clients.

Web Site: In this plugged-in era, an Internet presence is crucial to legitimizing your brand. It's not only a fabulous medium for presenting a business and reaching a larger audience, it's invaluable in a day and age when people are more likely to search for a service on Google than in the

Yellow Pages. Even if the budget can't accommodate Web site design just yet, consider creating a blog using a free service such as Blogger.com or Wordpress.com.

Business Cards: There's nothing more frustrating than having a great conversation about your business venture and then not being able to furnish a card when asked. A business card is the simplest form of branding. It's imperative you and anyone working for you always have one at the ready.

Logo: From McDonald's golden arches to the Nike swoosh, logos play an important role in helping the public identify a brand in the blink of an eye. The best ones tend to be simple, yet memorable, so be thoughtful about what image will represent your business most successfully. You may also consider working with a graphic designer or artist to establish a fine-tuned logo that can be used for stationery, business cards, Web site, and brochures.

Marketing Materials: Brochures or advertisements should follow the tone set by your Web site and logo. Be sure not to sacrifice professionalism for the sake of flashiness.

Be Consistent

In all phases of your life, your image needs to be consistent with:

Your Vision and Values. Where do you want to be five years from now? Dress for it. People want to know where you are going in life. Be true to your values, accumulated from what you have learned from your parents, teachers, religious leaders, or other influential or powerful people. Do not equivocate.

Your Verbal and Non-verbal Communication. Make sure your body and mouth speak the same language. Always think about your gestures, your posture, and your smile. At least in Western culture, remember to look people in the eye when you speak with them.

Your Environment. Don't have a sloppy office; it reflects who you are and your co-workers or clients will wonder if you treat their business in a sloppy way. Don't drive a dirty car, filled with junk. You never know who is going to walk you to your car and you don't want to be perceived as a slob.

Your Corporate Identity. Represent your company. Be proud to be part of it. Represent your company's mission statement.

Your Own Brand. Be true to yourself. Stand out from the crowd.

Your Skills and Talents. You've been educated; you have a list of accomplishments. Make sure people perceive your level of accomplishments when they meet you.

Dress and Appearance

My mother always said, "You never get a second chance to make a first impression." She has a way of being right most of the time. Is that something that happens when you become a mom?

It takes a few seconds to make a negative impression and a lifetime to overcome one. In business, if your first impression goes badly, you may not get the opportunity for a second. It may not seem fair, but it is the truth. Before you ever open your mouth, you create an impression of yourself in the other person's mind. You need to be impeccably groomed and look your best at all times.

A study conducted in the 1980s by Dr. Albert Mehrabian at UCLA showed that 55% of how people judge you is based on what they see, 7% is based on the words they hear (the content of your message), and 38% is on the tone of your voice.

Make sure you are always perfectly groomed, no matter where you are going. You don't need to get dressed up to go to the grocery store, but show self-respect. Being groomed shows you have respect for yourself and for others. You may run out of the house looking like a bum thinking you won't run into anyone you know, but you could run into anyone. It can happen. Sometimes people see you and you don't even see them. You don't want them to misjudge you. Pay attention to your hair, facial hair or makeup, clothes, jewelry, shoes, socks, and hosiery.

The common sense point: A good first impression is necessary for creating positive personal impact. That's why it's important to take the time to look your best every day. Business etiquette and protocol expert Lydia Ramsey, author of *Manners That Sell*, says, "The day you decide to dress down or compromise your appearance may be the day that you are introduced to that all-important person whom you have been trying to meet for months."

The Importance of Color

The first thing we notice when we see someone is color. Are you wearing the right colors? There are two ways to look at color:

1. What colors flatter you?

2. The psychology of color.

So you love to wear black. I understand. It's easy, it's slimming, and it goes with everything. But is it your color? Do you get a lot of compliments when you wear black? At one time in my career, I wore a lot of black so I would be taken seriously. I never received many compliments, except when I wore other colors. I finally got the message. I experimented with different colors in department stores and realized I looked much better wearing warm autumn colors. I started wearing dark brown and charcoal as my power colors and started getting compliments again.

As psychologists have known for ages, color affects mood, apparent body shape, apparent age, your outlook on life, and the overall impression you make. Wearing your best range of colors can make you look younger, healthier, vibrant, and energetic. Wearing unflattering colors can make you look older, ill, exhausted, or dull.

The most credible colors in business are charcoal gray and navy blue. Why? They denote credibility and trustworthiness. Red is a power color. It denotes confidence, power, and passion. Earth tones are perceived as friendly and approachable. If you are networking and want to "work the room," wear brown, ecru, beige, or greige (combination of gray and beige). You will look more approachable than if you wear black.

Express Your Style

Style is not about beauty, age, size, wealth, or even fashion. It's about knowing and respecting yourself for who you are and having the confidence to discover and project your unique style in a consistent and confident manner. Sounds simple, doesn't it?

Style is how you express yourself. Not only the way you dress, but also how you talk, move your body, or do anything for that matter. A sense of style is often innate, but it can be learned. Think of people you admire, or people often in the news, e.g. Michelle Obama, Donald Trump, Paris Hilton, and Gordon Brown. Do you discern their sense of style? What does their style — or lack thereof — convey about them?

My classic female style examples are Grace Kelly, Audrey Hepburn, and Jackie Onassis. Carolina Herrera, the Venezuelan haute couture designer, represents style for me today, as does Posh Spice Victoria Beckham. Contemporary male examples are George Clooney (always well-dressed, big smile, clean-cut) and French President Nicolas Sarkozy.

Proportion and Fit

You may pay a thousand dollars for a suit, but if it doesn't fit properly, you will not make the impression you want. Good fit is essential for clothes to be worn well for a long time.

Good fit does not always mean paying more, but having a good tailor is important. Not many people can buy clothes off the rack and wear them without alterations. Designers do not seem to make clothes for real women, curves and all. It behooves women to find a good tailor. You can drop off pants at the dry cleaner if they need a hem, or a shirt if the sleeves need shortening; however, for jackets, suit pants, and outfits for dressier functions, find a good tailor. Depending on your body shape, you may need to have the shoulders taken in on every jacket to get the best look. For such delicate work, you will want to be confident of the tailor's experience.

Men are more fortunate. Sizes are fairly consistent from designer to designer and brand to brand. Another plus: When men purchase a suit, a pair of pants or a jacket, there is usually a tailor on staff who can make alterations in the store.

Mark Twain once said, "Clothes make the man [or woman]. Naked people have little or no influence on society." How right he was!

Clothes help us make that positive impression we all want. They help us look better than we are; they help accentuate the positive and play down the negative.

Your clothes shouldn't be like a second skin; they should fit close enough to look good but not reveal every bump and lump. On the other hand, baggy clothing is most definitely not flattering either. It will make you look sloppy and not create a good impression. Try to get something between too loose and too tight. Just skimming the body is ideal.

Scale, balance, and proportion are also important. If you are small, do not wear accessories or prints that are too big. They will walk in the door before you do, making you disappear! On the other hand, many of my plus-size clients have a tendency to wear a small gold chain around their neck or just a pair of stud earrings. Why bother? The jewelry will disappear. Everything you wear needs to be in proportion to your size. I am tall and always make sure my accessories are medium to large because I can pull it off. If I were to wear dainty jewelry, it would get lost.

Three Forms of Etiquette

There are three forms of etiquette, and all are important to moving up in the world.

Dining Etiquette

Table manners play an important part in making a favorable impression, yet they seem to have fallen by the wayside in this era of fast food and more casual dining standards. Don't let your own table behavior reflect this unhappy trend, as proper dining etiquette is a talent that can positively affect your future and your reputation.

Here's why: More and more employers are interviewing candidates over lunch or dinner. One of the reasons is so an employer can evaluate candidates' social skills firsthand and see if they can handle themselves gracefully under pressure. In other words, good manners may give you the edge over another candidate.

Do you feel comfortable with the way you eat? Do you eat American or Continental style? Which is your bread dish? How do you pass food to your tablemates? How about salt and pepper? Did you know that when someone asks you to pass the salt, you must pass both the salt and the pepper? Yes, they are "married"!

Social Etiquette

What is the correct way to sneeze or cough in public? (To avoid spreading germs, sneeze or cough into your sleeve or elbow, not your hand.)

Should you pull out a chair for a woman when she is sitting down for dinner? (Yes.)

Do you know when to get on or off an elevator? (Wait for everyone to get off before you get on.)

Should you introduce your boss to your client or your client to your boss? Who is more important? (Always introduce the more important person to the less important person. In a business environment, the client is more important than the boss, so introduce your client to your boss.)

Do you know how or to whom to send thank-you notes? Do you know what to say in them? Send a handwritten thank-you note by regular mail to everyone who has given or sent you something, or done something for you. The note should be brief and consist of four parts: 1) the salutation; 2) your appreciation for the gift or gesture, mentioning how much you like it or have enjoyed it; 3) a suggestion for a future meeting; 4) the closing. And remember to keep a supply of appropriate commemorative postage stamps on hand.

Business Etiquette

With the advent of technology, business etiquette no longer includes only how to write a business letter or address your boss. Business etiquette now also covers tech etiquette, or "netiquette." It includes e-mail, cellphones, texting, voice mail, and social networks.

Think of your e-mail as you might your business card. Does it look tasteful and professional? Does it provide pertinent contact information? Write your e-mail as a business letter. Always use a salutation, check the spelling and punctuation, and make sure you have a closing (e.g. "sincerely" or "best regards"). Have all your contact information in your signature so people don't need to search for your telephone number if they want to call rather than e-mail. Steer clear of jazzing up your e-mail with colorful text, dark backgrounds, or cutesy graphics. They are distracting and undermine your professional image.

Texting has also become an increasingly common way to communicate. Text messaging has spawned an egregious lapse of proper language skills that can seriously hamper your professional image. I don't recommend that you text anyone but friends and family. Texting is not professional. It implies a certain casual intimacy that may not be appropriate with a work colleague, and certainly not your boss.

The most important advice I can give you? Do not multi-task! It is very rude. Do not check your e-mail while in a meeting. It shows a lack of respect for the person conducting the meeting. Do not answer your cellphone when you are with a client. You want to make the person you are with know that they are the most important person at the time. The only exception would be if you expect an important call. In this rare case, let your client know ahead of time. Should you receive the call, excuse yourself, go to another room, and make the conversation short. When you return to your meeting or the table, thank them for their understanding.

Social Media

Social media are here to say. These are no longer something just for high school or college students.

The fastest-growing Facebook demographic in mid-2009 was the 35-and-older age group, with the 35-to-54 segment accelerating at a 276.4% growth rate in the first half of the year.

LinkedIn, at the same time, had more than 41 million members in 200 countries and territories around the world (half outside the United States) and reported that a new member was joining at a rate of about one every second. Executives from all Fortune 500 companies are LinkedIn members.

LinkedIn helps you make better use of your professional network of trusted contacts and is one of your most valuable assets. Used properly, it can help connect the world's professionals to accelerate their success. The important caveat is "if used properly."

Be guided by this: Don't post anything you would not want your mother to see; that guidance should, in fact, be the standard for all your behavior in the business world.

More on Branding

What is the difference between a company brand and me as a brand?

Angela: Think of Coca-Cola and Pepsi or UPS and FedEx. These brands do not rely on the face or name of an individual, and management changes do not cause a drop in business. In a startup, though, the owner is the brand. People do business with you because of you. That can change.

At first you know all the customers and they know you. Then employees may be hired to handle some customers. After more growth, you may only know the large accounts. The time could come when you don't know any of the customers and no longer are the face of the company. At that point, new customers are being attracted for another reason and your branding has changed.

Marla: I try to meet and personally talk with each of my clients so they know the person they are doing business with. In the medical spa business, I am a reflection of the brand. People decide what my business and culture is like based upon how I look and act.

Eleanor: If you provide a service that cannot be replicated by anyone else in your company, the business is limited to marketing your skills. If you want to train others to provide the service, you should start branding the company's service, not yours. This allows the business to continue past your exit.

How can I market myself when I am the brand?

Marla: In my business, marketing means I must take good care of my skin and body. We sell packages to eliminate cellulite, hair, wrinkles, and age spots. I must use the services and products I sell. When customers come in, they look at my staff and me to decide whether they want to spend their money. Part of this decision is based on their perception of how well we take care of ourselves. This proves we are "walking the walk."

Angela: Setting up a Web site was one way I could show what I did for other companies and make it easy for prospective clients to view it at their convenience. It is not uncommon for people to say, "Oh, I love your site. I noticed you did something I want. Can you do that for me, even if it is a different industry?" Because I am a writer and designer, I make sure my marketing materials, including my business card, are consistent and interesting. When I got confident enough, I showed my face. I was differentiating myself from competitors; it worked.

When I started including photos on my Web site, business cards, and other marketing materials, things started happening — for the better. I believe it was because there was a friendly face customers could relate to. Since I am a technician — I sell knowledge and expertise — this is proving even more important for me than, say, it would be for a chain of car dealerships to show the owner's face.

Peggy: And remember: Be yourself, your perfect image, consistently, 24/7, everywhere and anywhere.

How can I determine my company's message or tagline?

Marla: A tagline should emphasize your specialty, show what makes you unique, and help people quickly understand what you are about — all in one line. Catchy phrases help customers remember you when they have a need. My company's taglines are Treat Yourself to the Very Best and Everyone Deserves to Feel Beautiful.

Peggy: Listen to what satisfied clients say. Combine that with what you want to convey to the world, and make it simple and clear. My tagline is We Help Individuals Create the BEST Version of Themselves.

Eleanor: Compare what your company does and how it is serving the marketplace to the message or tagline you are considering. Company names (such as ours at MD&E, Inc.) do not always provide information that allows the marketplace to know what service you provide. So you use a tagline to provide that information. Taglines can change based upon growth or diversification. For instance, our tagline now is Tactical Solutions for Business. As of this writing, however, we just finished developing our new branding, Clarity CRM Specialists, with the tagline Making Data Make Money.

Angela: I used a quotation thesaurus and looked up all quotations dealing with my lines of work — marketing, advertising, and writing. The book gave me great ideas and I settled on one that, to this day, is popular with customers. My company's tagline is Is Your Business Winking in the Dark? It is based on this quote by Steuart Henderson Britt: "Doing business without advertising is like winking at a girl in the dark. You know what you are doing, but nobody else does." I have used this quote so long it has been attributed to me in the press.

How can I make sure my company's message is consistent?

Marla: First build a marketing strategy and then tailor the message.

Eleanor: Make the message consistent throughout all communications, inside and outside the company, including the Web site, press releases, collateral materials, and customer- and employee-focused newsletters. As the owner, you are responsible for the company's message being expressed properly by everyone who represents your company.

Angela: If you do not have a logo, get one. But don't take it from some other business or copy one from an online source. Think ahead. Just because you are small now does not mean you will always be. If the company grows and the logo gets out into the wider world, somebody somewhere will be after you legally for stealing their logo. Create, don't copy.

Peggy: And be sure to "walk the walk." As I said before, you cannot profess to be one thing and do the opposite in your private life; you will eventually be found out. Control the message. If others control it for you, you may not like the results.

Do I really need a Web site?

Marla: The Internet is the way people do business today. If you do not have a Web site, you prevent yourself from growing beyond the physical reach you have in a community. You also may look old school to a consumer who is technologically savvy. A Web site is one of the most cost-effective ways to market and communicate with potential clients.

Peggy: How else are you going to market yourself? Some people prefer blogs over Web sites, but I don't agree. A site gives you more exposure; you can use video and audio to explain what you do. You can display testimonials. The sky is the limit. However, a blog is a nice companion to a site, and you should make consistent use of at least one social network, the one most frequented by prospective clients.

Eleanor: The company Web site is the face of the organization. Since it often is a customer's first impression, it is important that the site be professional and current as well as represent what the company does.

Angela: Some businesses do not need them. Case in point: I have a friend who, together with her husband, has a small business performing lawn care and landscaping for small businesses. They handle about five clients and want no more. But that's an exception. For most businesses, having a site — even one merely for informational purposes — can introduce you to a wider audience and position you favorably in the marketplace. Don't let it look sloppy. Don't have hard-to-read fonts. Don't use loud colors. And for goodness' sake, don't have a distracting background. Those things turn off customers.

How important are business cards, logos, and other marketing materials?

Angela: As energetic as you might be, you cannot be all places at all times. Your card in a Rolodex or drawer needs to jump out from those surrounding it. Please don't use the free business cards you can order online with the name of another business on the back. Really, if you do not want to invest in your own business, why should a customer spend money with you?

Peggy: Money spent on promotional materials is well spent. They are your company's Public Relations and Marketing Department.

Eleanor: Keeping the messaging and the imaging consistent extends the brand. Keep it professional.

Marla: The only downside to all these things is that printed materials can become costly. I chose a logo for my medical spa that projected an image of class, beauty, and professionalism. I have service menus, fancy bags for products, customized chocolates, business cards, plush robes and wraps, a customized product line, and exquisite gold boxes for gift certificates, each with our logo. As the customer receives one after the other, her expectations are heightened about who we are and what she can hope to experience in our upscale environment.

How can I expand marketing opportunities?

Angela: If your clients tend to be in a particular industry, consider joining an association for that industry.

Peggy: Join organizations whose members you would like to have as clients. Attend conferences and trade shows. Sponsor events.

Eleanor: Joining the right organizations is helpful from a business standpoint. Spend time looking at the makeup of the membership, the goals and aspirations of the group, and the level of participation before joining. Pick the ones that give a greater return on your time investment.

Chambers of Commerce are good for meeting other business owners as well as a pipeline to knowing when new businesses are coming. Knowing the issues of other businesses helps you be aware of the items all of you are facing collectively. Chambers are also a great networking opportunity. Women's organizations offer many opportunities to learn and network.

Marla: Every encounter with another person is a marketing opportunity. When I make a purchase or transaction, I take the opportunity to mention my business and what I do. Also consider non-traditional forms of marketing like blogs and social media such as LinkedIn, Facebook, and YouTube. Also consider buying premium online advertising.

How can I determine which organizations will work best for me?

Angela: Talk to other members and ask how they have benefited.

Peggy: Review your marketing plan regularly and adjust membership commitments accordingly. For example, if you have been a member of the same Chamber of Commerce for two years, been active on a committee, attended events, and yet have not made any useful business connections, it's time to move on and select another organization.

Chapter 10

Eleanor on Relationships
Relationships Q&A

RELATIONSHIPS IN BUSINESS

No woman is an island, nor should she want to be.

By Eleanor Morgan

There is no business without relationships.

MD&E, Inc., the Atlanta-based company I co-founded with my husband in 1994, is an $8 million IT firm with more than 80 employees. The long, intense process of building the company started with a single contract job. I was awarded that first contract because a good friend believed in my skills and took a chance on me.

As I look back at how we got here, I now — finally — recognize that relationships were, and continue to be, the single biggest common denominator in the journey.

Along the way, I gave liberally of my time and energy to help others, as well as myself, grow and develop. But personal and professional interactions took a back seat to building a career. At the time, they represented little more than steppingstones.

I achieved success through hard work, the grace of God, a loving husband, and the generous spirit of people I encountered along the way — people who shared their knowledge and skills and helped me develop my own. I have worked long and hard to help repay, in part, the gifts I received.

When I envision the paths my life has taken, I see them lined with family, friends, clients, and employees — all those who listened to my dreams and helped them come true through their generous gifts of time, trust, knowledge, and opportunity. Their very presence continues to enrich my life. I can only hope I have done the same for them.

Life would cease to have meaning, or even exist, without human connections. Yet too many of us treat our associations as afterthoughts or annoyances. We often don't give freely of our time and energy when we are shown love, loyalty, and devotion.

Self-development expert Dale Carnegie, explaining the insight behind his legendary book *How to Win Friends and Influence People*, said, "I realized that as surely as these adults needed training in effective speaking, they needed still more training in the fine art of getting along with people in everyday business and social contacts. I also gradually realized that I was sorely in need of such training myself…"

Mr. Carnegie recognized not only the importance of social skills in every aspect of modern life but also the difficulty of learning — and especially practicing — those skills. "Dealing with people is probably the biggest problem you face, especially if you are in business," he wrote. "…And that is also true if you are a housewife, architect or engineer."

Who we are is determined by how we view the world and how that view shapes our behavior. I don't generally view social interaction as a problem. I genuinely like people and enjoy their company, and believe that people whose behavior causes problems are the exception rather than the rule.

Still, I wholeheartedly agree with the remainder of Mr. Carnegie's assessment. Relationships are the single most important ingredient of a successful and satisfying business, not to mention a successful and satisfying life.

Relationships, however, don't just happen. Even the most promising initial meeting cannot develop into a full-fledged relationship without a significant investment of time, energy, and sincerity on the part of both people. A seed may be perfect and ripe with promise and potential, but without consistent care and nourishment it will never grow, and its potential will never be realized.

Business relationships come in all shapes and sizes. They might include associations with colleagues, competitors, customers, vendors, suppliers, neighbors, regulators, co-workers, bosses, partners, and employees, to name the most obvious examples.

There is no escaping these interactions, even for the most self-reliant or anti-social among us. By definition, no business can subsist on a single-person basis. Even a sole proprietor must have external affiliations to survive, much less succeed.

Then there are personal relationships — those that family, friends, school, church and other people, groups, or places bring to your life — and the threads and influences they weave through all your business and other relationships. These relationships may be harder to pigeonhole or define, but they are intensely important to quality of life. Family, friends, and faith have forged unbreakable, invaluable relationships that have played integral roles in who I am, how I developed, even how I do business.

You Are Your Most Important Teacher

I continue to learn from others. From reading incessantly, attending workshops and seminars, and spending countless hours in front of my PC to learn what I need to know, I try to determine what works and what doesn't. I am always asking myself how to make things work better.

While all this study helped, the most valuable knowledge has come from my eagerness to learn about people and how to build lasting relationships.

Being a business owner means selling your expertise — your ability to satisfy client needs by providing services and/or products superior to the competition's. But beware: Expertise is a voracious and demanding companion; it must be fed well — and often — or it will desert you, often at the moment you need it most. Since your expertise is your livelihood, you must continue to develop your skills. Take time to read. Seek out experts and learn from them. Be involved in groups that challenge you to grow in existing areas and create new areas of expertise. You may also need to bring others into your business to supplement some of these areas.

Make an effort to keep your mind open; don't just hear, listen — and listen again — to the advice, experiences, and opinions of others. Patiently consider the information, analyze its relevance to you, and carefully weigh how this information might help you in business or personal development.

Make Every Employee Matter

The clash of the old guard and the new is not a recent development. Henry Ford acknowledged it early in the last century, saying, "A company needs smart young men with the imagination and the guts to turn everything upside down if they can. It also needs old figures to keep them from turning upside down those things that ought to be right side up."

Whether an employee is young or old, new hire or seasoned veteran, it is important to the health, stability, and future of your business to share what you have learned with each one.

This simple, top-down communication is the most effective way of proving to employees that they are not disposable, interchangeable hired hands but valued partners in a team effort. It helps improve their performance, builds and strengthens loyalty, and converts the traditional employee-management structure — with all its inherent, unspoken resentments and class distinctions — into a collaborative environment.

When you make it a point to consistently relate to employees as individuals, it allows them to recognize their importance in your eyes and helps them believe more strongly in their jobs, their company, and themselves. Employees who believe in themselves can become the individuals they were created to be and reach their full — all-too-often untapped — potential.

Seek Relationships, Share Your Knowledge

While the office provides numerous opportunities for learning, it isn't the only classroom outside the academic institution. Students, like teachers, can be found anywhere.

Business owners should actively seek opportunities to share their experiences with people outside their employ. Help a friend, lead a seminar, join a professional group; do whatever it takes to teach and to learn. All of these things will make you a better business owner and a better person.

Knowledge is like a classic work of art — its true value is evident only when shared. I have worked with many individuals outside my company to help prepare them for a special event or major change in their business or personal lives. I am excited by the opportunity to offer any wisdom I might have to help make their lives better, more fulfilling, or more successful.

Nurture Business Relationships

Relationships do not form instantly. Sharing experiences and memories, either individually or in groups in and out of the office, creates bonds that can be called upon at appropriate times.

One excellent, and much-appreciated, method is to pitch in and share the burden of heavy workloads with your employees rather than standing back in a classic "I manage; you work" stance and letting the weight fall on them alone.

Preparing to launch a new client program is a long, arduous process that often requires night and weekend work. Rather than relax at home during these marathon sessions, I made it a point to lend a hand. I handled basic or routine tasks, provided coffee and snacks, and even drove employees home when they worked into the wee hours of the morning.

Such experiences provide special opportunities to build relationships and to know employees that typical 8-to-5 schedules cannot allow. Handing down orders and voicing "good job" platitudes simply would not work, so I put myself on the front lines, demonstrating support for their efforts.

They repaid me many times over with their loyalty and consistently top-grade performance.

My employees often tell me I treat them like family, and I am gratified by that. In many ways, my employees are like family; I have seen them grow up, marry, become parents, become successful, and give back to the community. I have celebrated the births of their children with them and watched with pride as the children grew. I have shared their joys and sorrows; they, in turn, have shared mine. I would not have it any other way.

True to our family-type relationship, our Norcross, Georgia, building is a magnificent old renovated home. During our first holiday season there, Santa and Mrs. Claus graciously agreed to take time from their busy schedules to fly in for a visit as we decorated. We invited our employees and their families to join the celebration. Their children's faces beamed with beautiful, joyous smiles, and their voices buzzed with the excitement and anticipation only Christmas can generate.

As I watched, I thought about how our company helped provide for each and every one of those children. But that warm, wonderful feeling was also somehow frightening. I had thought 75 to 100 employees depended on our company. Suddenly I realized it was not just employees counting on our success, but also their families — a total of around 300 people. It's a huge responsibility, one I take seriously.

My dream, my hope, my wish is that my company will continue to grow and succeed so those children will continue to visit us on those happy holidays, and that they will one day have the opportunity to work here and remain part our business family, if they so desire.

I cannot imagine a better legacy.

Go for the Gold in Employee Relationships

Every business owner cares about their company. If you are like most, you also care about the satisfaction and success of your employees. But do they know that? Many owners discover to their dismay that effectively communicating that care to employees takes time, commitment, and — sometimes — a failure or two to be successful. If you can't be successful in communicating your appreciation, concern, and satisfaction to your employees, how can you expect your employees to reciprocate?

If you think being a strong, competent boss is enough to get the job done, and that soliciting active employee investment in the company's vision, goals, and objectives isn't necessary, you are only fooling yourself. You are only one person. You can't do it all.

If you ignore these basics of decent human behavior, the other actions you take or words you speak will never carry their true weight of meaning, no matter how well-intended. If you master the basics, even the little things you do for employees will pack a big punch.

Our company performs contract jobs for large corporations. Many projects require us to work on-site, so we regularly operate out of barely adequate makeshift accommodations.

My employees tell me it meant a lot when I made an effort to transform these uninviting spots into more pleasant workspaces by moving file cabinets, hanging pictures, bringing in lamps, or making other small gestures. They also let me know they enjoyed the cards, candy, and little souvenirs I left on their desks from time to time. The true gift, of course, was not the gestures but the employees' realization that I am thinking about them and showing appreciation for their hard work.

Building Your Business Team

Most of us like working with people similar to us, but business owners and managers should resist the temptation to hire only people who match them closely in personality, background, or attitude, or who always agree with their opinions and decisions.

Hiring clones does not reinforce your team's strengths but instead exposes weaknesses by reducing the ability to be flexible.

Eleanor's Tips

Examples of positive and negative interactions and the usual results:

Positive Action: Showing you care by doing your job as owner or manager, and doing it well. Demonstrate competence by addressing issues and resolving problems affecting employees. Set a strong example.

Outcome: Employees respect you and work to become more valuable.

Positive Action: Asking for active assistance in achieving the company's visions, keeping its values, and reaching its goals and objectives.

Outcome: Employees understand and share your vision, values, goals, and objectives.

Positive Action: Regularly communicating the company's goals and objectives. Encourage sharing in the ownership of these ideals.

Outcome: Employees' involvement grows.

Positive Action: Allowing employees to help the business grow.

Outcome: Employees become salespeople for your company.

Positive Action: Treating others as you would like to be treated. This simple piece of advice goes a long way.

Outcome: Employees feel valued.

Positive Action: Considering how your actions or words make others feel.

Outcome: Employees begin to understand you care about their welfare.

Negative Action: Failing to address issues and resolve problems affecting employees.

Outcome: Employees lose faith in your ability to lead. They may find other role models, possibly negative ones, within the company.

Negative Action: Not including employees in discussions about vision and goals.

Outcome: They will not be able to support your decisions and objectives. Also, you lose valuable input.

Negative Action: Not allowing employees to be involved in business growth and success.

Outcome: You stifle growth for each as they attempt to become a part of that success.

Negative Action: Not treating others with respect.

Outcome: Employees will not support you and will not see the need to respect others, including fellow employees and customers.

Negative Action: Not considering your actions or words.

Outcome: You create hurt feelings and loss of trust, losing valuable employees.

Your team needs to think in different ways. Involving too many like-thinking people hampers your ability to embrace new ideas that solve problems outside existing processes.

An exception would be when hiring someone who might replace you; you would want them to share the values and thought processes you used to successfully grow the business. Even in this case, you should look for new ideas and the ability to think outside existing processes.

Some people confuse disagreement with confrontation, leading to don't-rock-the-boat thinking. To avoid what they consider unpleasantness, they end up stagnating their business. More than one company has folded because its managers would not, could not, and did not challenge the status quo and change to meet the market.

However, when a healthy range of opinion is sought and challenges to current thinking are raised and met, the process results in solid business decisions. You create a dynamic, strong, and progressive business that will continue to produce solutions for customers.

Do not be afraid to hire people smarter than you. The most successful, forward-thinking entrepreneurs are not intimidated by employees with bigger and better ideas. They wisely do not allow personal insecurities to dissuade them from strengthening the intellectual and creative capacities of their companies.

The faith you place in all employees makes them more loyal and devoted. And if you don't snap up gifted people, the competition will. Astute owners seek out people smarter than themselves.

Your Personal Team

Until now, the focus has been on office teams. But personal teams are just as vital. Building a business is rewarding but also stressful and exhausting. It can take a serious toll on you and your family's health and happiness.

Good friendships, what I like to call "personal teams," provide an outlet for negatives such as customer complaints, disciplining employees, losing a proposal to a competitor, or having a key employee resign.

If you carry these problems home it disrupts your family and drains your personal life of joy.

In my story, I mentioned my first customer's employees, who were willing and helpful enough to teach me the ropes of the corporate environment. Some of my relationships with those colleagues were born in the office but did not end there. They grew into strong, nurturing friendships that continue today. We stay in touch, travel together, and spend time helping each other solve problems.

These are strong, compassionate women who know me well and aren't afraid to give me their honest viewpoint. I know them just as well and do the same for them. We all benefit, personally and professionally.

Not all friendships lend themselves to this type of interaction. Just as office teams need the proper mix of personalities and temperaments, so do personal teams. Don't assume office friends always work as personal friends. Errors in judgment can have a negative impact in both areas. If you place your trust in an undeserving friend from the office, private conversations may well be used to their benefit. Think carefully before choosing employees or customers as personal friends.

When you make it a point to seek out friends who provide emotional support and offer ideas that challenge you to grow outside your comfort zone, it allows you to validate your own thoughts or perhaps see things differently, providing a growth opportunity. A good way to do this is to get acquainted with people in professional organizations. They can be your sounding board.

Other areas in which to grow relationships outside of work are neighborhood or charitable groups. These allow you to give back to your community. You will find that common interests often provide a good foundation for a rewarding friendship.

Personal teams also create avenues to connect with those who can provide support for you and the business. Just as I found opportunities for work from neighbors, friends, and church members, I have been able to provide such opportunities to others.

It is amazing how the relationships you experience throughout life can dovetail in so many unexpected — and unexpectedly rewarding — ways. In essence, good relationships make the difference between stagnation and opportunity, discontent and happiness, and frustration and success in your personal and professional life.

An opportunity to form a meaningful relationship is a door to possibilities that can literally change your life. Enjoy where these opportunities take you.

More on Relationships

My business is just me. Do I really need to know about team- building?

Eleanor: It is important to learn these skills for customer, vendor, and personal interactions. Together a group of people can accomplish much more than an individual. Having this skill helps in all areas of life.

Angela: Even if you have no employees, like in my print brokering business, you have vendors who need motivating so that you, in turn, can take care of customers. You may also have to deal with a group of people at the customer's location. They may look to you to tell them what to do or help clarify a plan. If you let personalities get in the way and do not know how to react to and motivate each one, you will not improve the situation. Learn how to influence and build.

How can I focus my employees on acting like a team?

Eleanor: Along with being a trailblazer in cartooning, motion pictures, television, and theme parks, Walt Disney was also a pioneer in what we now know as team-building. The Disney team built the Disney brand. When asked to rank his many accomplishments, Mr. Disney replied, "Of all the things I've done, the most vital is coordinating the talents of those who work for us and pointing them towards a certain goal."

Yet some people believe all you need to do to build a great team is throw money at talented people and put them in the same room. Building a winning team requires more. The ingredient that pulls things together is your passion and the willingness to share it. Passion spreads energy from the leader into every employee, producing a shared purpose and the will to win.

Some employees grow out of positions and need to move on for their own development. Some never share the passion required to be a part of the team. Knowing the individuals allows you to do what is best for them and the company. Assess and assign the proper mix of personalities to meet individual and company needs. Real people are complex and contradictory, their situations multi-faceted. Understanding is critical. When needs are not addressed and a satisfactory solution reached, the situation can fester into dissatisfaction, frustration, or animosity.

Go with your gut. You should have the most complete understanding of all the business and personal elements involved, giving you an instinctive feeling of what's right for everyone. Your gut may not always be completely correct, but rarely is it completely wrong.

Never go into a meeting or a major decision without complete knowledge of the goals and an understanding of what motivates the individuals involved, and thus the group as a whole.

Marla: My team, and the culture they create at my medical spa, is my single greatest asset. Clients always comment about the quality of my team and how wonderful they make customers feel. As the owner, it is important to set the appropriate tone and expectations for the staff.

How can I determine whether I would be a good mentor?

Angela: Are you willing to share whatever knowledge you have and spend time with those who may not be able to benefit you financially? If so, you are mentor material.

Marla: I learned a valuable lesson in Corporate America. If people follow you only because of your title, you are simply a manager. If people follow you regardless of your title, you are a leader. Leaders are the people who make the best mentors. You are always an informal mentor to people you meet and employ.

Eleanor: The greatest lessons can come from people who may find it ironic to be counted among your educators because they didn't think they knew anything of value. I have learned valuable lessons from neighbors, bosses, co-workers, employees, and friends.

I am mentor material. How can I start?

Eleanor: Share what you learned. In my business, young employees arrive knowing the latest software inside out but are ill-equipped to handle difficult clients or competing deadlines. My role as a mentor is to identify the knowledge gap, help others develop the skills, and guide them in channeling what they offer in the often-illogical world of human business relationships.

Marla: Make it a goal to help others succeed. Success breeds success. There can be nothing more fulfilling in life than to help others learn and grow.

Angela: When people ask for advice, take the time to thoughtfully answer their questions. Then take it a step further. Answer a question they did not think to ask but one that is important to their education in the matter.

What is required of someone who is mentored?

Peggy: An open mind, an eagerness to learn, an unwavering commitment, a zeal for success.

Angela: The willingness to listen and ask for clarifying information.

Eleanor: If you are not offered instruction, ask for it. Seek out the knowledge you need to progress. Whether you work for a large corporation, a small business, or yourself, one of the worst mistakes is to assume you know it all. The first thing a truly intelligent person admits is there is always more to learn.

Marla: Gratitude. Recognize and receive mentorship as a gift.

How can I identify a mentor for me?

Angela: Ask a lot of questions. When you find someone who slows down, answers you, and then offers more, it is a sure bet you have found the person you need.

Eleanor: Who do you know that is blessed with skills and knowledge that can help you grow professionally or personally? Take advantage of opportunities to learn. Keep the passion for learning alive by feeding it regularly. Never underestimate the value of the information or advice someone might offer.

Marla: The right person usually finds you. An effective mentor recognizes a need and truly wants to help. Keep your eyes open for him or her. Mentors come in forms we may not expect or anticipate.

Chapter 11

Eleanor and Angela
on Family Businesses

Owning — and Surviving — a Family Business

By Eleanor Morgan

It is natural to want your child to work in the family business. You're proud of both. Who's better qualified for stewardship of your legacy?

There are dozens of reasons to hire your children — and thousands of horror stories that compel us to first examine the downside of such arrangements.

Having children in the family business leaves no space between lives. At family events, it is easy for the conversations to be more about business than personal matters. The lines can blur between who you are and what you do.

An employee/child must believe in the dream of growing the business or it won't be possible for him or her to step into your shoes. There must be a fit. The business needs to suit the child's skills and personality, especially if it is service-oriented. It takes personality to constantly interact with people.

Blended families have special issues no matter how good the relationship between child and stepparent. Sometimes favorites are played or special alliances are made, benefiting neither family nor company.

Children in the same business can feel overshadowed by a parent's success. Elsewhere in the company, the best and most loyal employees can feel their opportunities are strangled by family ties.

Then there's the matter of working in the same company with your spouse. Wonderful husbands do what wonderful husbands do best: try to protect the ones they love. My wonderful husband at first tried to protect me from hard business decisions by stepping in to handle them; it didn't allow me to grow as a business owner.

Conversations meant to release anger, frustration, or hurt turned into problem-solving discussions because a husband wants to protect. When all I needed was someone to vent to about my day, he tried to take the problem away. When I needed to talk through how to solve it, he would wonder why I didn't just let him handle it.

Eventually we came to an understanding.

Husbands and wives are a team and can develop each other. Bonding at work can bring them closer — if they let it. They can be a strong team with different skill sets complementing each other's strengths. This balance is a powerful asset in your business and your personal life.

For children, that bonding can be part of an education in life skills, as well as a chance to earn a salary maybe not possible in an entry-level job.

Working for a parent as a boss encourages children to negotiate for what they feel needs to happen with the business. They learn to gain agreement — or agree to disagree.

Valuable leadership skills can be developed. As you share reasons for big-picture decisions, children learn more about decisions and leadership in a parent's company than in any other.

Children see you work hard, which is good and bad. They may decide the cost of leadership is too high. Sometimes children see hard work as something that takes attention away from them and may resent the amount of time it takes you to build a business.

They see your heart and passion, how you treat others, and how it turns out. They watch your actions toward employees and customers to see if you really live up to the things you tell them about integrity.

Now it is time to reveal how this played out in my business.

Our consulting company, which specializes in system data, at one point employed my husband's son and daughter, son-in-law, and daughter-in-law, plus a brother to the daughter-in-law. Add in my daughter and our lives all revolved around the business and relationships developed there.

It was an exciting yet difficult time as we were building the business and trying to involve our children. After five years with lots of family involved, we now have only myself working daily with my husband's support. The others have moved into areas that allow them to have passion for what they are doing. This allows each of these treasured people in my life to grow into the person they are intended to be.

Their experiences working for MD&E, Inc. will hopefully make them more successful in their own ventures. My husband has moved into a role on our Board of Directors and continues to offer much-needed and appreciated advice about financial and marketing decisions.

For me, it is refreshing to get together as family and not have business be a part of our conversation at all. Family members' time working at MD&E provided a financial and growth opportunity that allowed each to move into creating their own legacy.

Let Junior Learn Elsewhere

By Angela K. Durden

If your business is family-owned or -operated, are your children growing up in the business? If yes, do you want your grown children to eventually take over day-to-day operations? Then you will want to properly prepare the next generation for their role in what will one day become their business.

Rodney Dangerfield was famous for saying "I get no respect." While his saying was shtick, many children of business owners often feel that way when they work for Mom or Dad — and for good reason. Often Mommy or Daddy gave Junior a job and probably protected him from the harsh realities of meeting a deadline or making forecast. So Junior doesn't have a clue why no one respects him in what will one day surely be his business. That is why it is important to let another business train Junior.

Let him cut his business teeth (and make the mistakes!) while working for someone else. If you give him an opportunity to gain confidence, you will defuse the potential for ridicule by non-family employees. Furthermore, when Junior does come to work for you, let him do so only if he has a genuine interest in the business and can make real contributions in a position that truly exists and has performance standards to be met. Therefore, always have Junior fill a real position.

Also, make Junior earn his keep just like everyone else. No inflated salary just because he is related. Be prepared to pay on merit. If the company offers a family bonus, keep it separate from the other pay schedule.

A very wise person once said, "I never make the same mistake twice. It's more like three or four times." Therefore, a smart parent/business owner will allow Junior to make mistakes and learn from them, and will encourage employees to rate Junior's overall performance and give honest feedback, hints, and tips for improving.

Ever since Junior was born you planned for the day when he would take over the business. You imagined your chest filling with pride as you handed it over. But Junior may not be as enthused about your business as you are and would really prefer to do something else. Let him do so and you can both move on in a positive manner.

On the other hand, he may love the business just as much as you but have other ideas or fresh insights that may very well clash with yours. So what? Let Junior use his brain and try out new ideas. You did it when you started the business and look what fun you have had! Disagreements and differences of opinion about business should not a relationship break. But to make it easier to handle those differences, talk honestly about your long-term plans for the business and Junior's place in the business.

Don't let the duties, responsibilities, choices, and decisions blindside [your children] because of lack of knowledge and preparation. Educate and prepare the next generation for their upcoming role. You may establish a dynasty; or not. Either way, as you look back at the various stages of your life and business, are you happy with the positive role you have played in your family's and employees' lives? Take a moment to reflect. What is your answer? Is it what you would like it to be? If yes, then you are to be congratulated. If no, you still have time to make a difference.

Five Steps to a Smooth Family Business Transition

- Let another business train Junior.
- Have Junior fill a real position.
- Pay on merit.
- Encourage employees to rate Junior's overall performance and give honest feedback, hints, and tips for improving.
- Talk honestly about your long-term plans for the business and Junior's place in the business.

[This article first appeared in the UTA Industry Watch *in January 2007 (www.UTA.org). For more information on this topic, check out* 9 Elements of Family Business Success *by Allen Fishman.]*

Recommended Reading

Authors' Acknowledgements

Complete Quotes

Books the authors found useful in starting their businesses:

Angela: *Guerrilla Marketing* by Jay Conrad Levinson and *Crucial Conversations* by Kerry Patterson, Joseph Grenny, Ron McMillan, and Al Switzler.

Marla: *How Customers Think: Essential Insights Into the Mind of the Market* by Gerald Zaltman; *Think and Grow Rich* by Napoleon Hill; and *Just Business: Christian Ethics for the Marketplace* by Alexander Hill.

Peggy: *The E-Myth Revisited* by Michael E. Gerber; *Feel the Fear and Do It Anyway* by Susan Jeffers; *Little Black Book of Connections* by Jeffrey Gitomer; *Your Best Year Yet!* by Jinny S. Ditzler; *You've Only Got Three Seconds* by Camille Lavington; *Business Class* by Jacqueline Whitmore; and *First Impressions* by Ann Demarais and Valerie White.

Eleanor: *A Strategy for Winning* by Carl Mays; *A Leader's Legacy* by Jim Kouzes and Barry Posner; *Talent Is Never Enough* and *Winning With People,* both by John Maxwell; *Built to Last* by Jim Collins and Jerry I. Porras; *The Speed of Trust* by Stephen M. R. Covey; and *The Dream Giver* by Bruce Wilkinson.

Authors' Acknowledgements

Every book owes its tone, flavor, and organization to more than the authors. The process starts with truthful friends who read it over and over, giving much-needed feedback, and business associates and relatives who tell us what they want to read. Too numerous to list here, you know who you are, and we thank you.

Then there are the professionals, whose business is words and presentation. We must start with Jedwin Smith. A renowned author and veteran newspaperman, Jedwin knows how to tell a story. His first read-through of what we thought were our final drafts showed us where the holes were. We thank him for making our stories complete.

Then there is Bobbie Christmas. She went through our entire book line by line, giving us even more opportunities for improvement.

Jim Chatwin, our photographer, captured the best in us. Randi Chatwin, our makeup artist, brought out the best in us, making Jim's job even easier. (Jim knows that's true.)

Lastly, we all bow before the genius of Tom Whitfield, another veteran newspaperman and business editor. His keen insight into the content brought more clarity than we ever could have wished for. Tom's devotion to our project went above and beyond the call of duty. His organization of the how-to sections took a good effort and turned it into a thing of beauty. Thank you, Tom.

If there are any shortcomings in this book, you may blame us, because they were not due to the efforts of those around us.

Marla, Angela, Peggy, and Eleanor

Complete Quotes From Back Cover

Linda K. Wind
CEO & President, Wind Enterprises, Inc.
Founder, Wind Foundation for Women and Possible Woman Foundation

As an entrepreneur myself, I eagerly looked forward to reading Opportunity Meets Motivation, and it certainly did not disappoint.

Through my Possible Woman Leadership Conferences and events, I have met every possible shade of Angela, Eleanor, Marla, and Peggy — and then some! These stories are truly wonderful, written by real women who started businesses of their own and pursued success in their own distinct ways. Their advice, contained in this book, encourages those women following in their footsteps to jump in and take the entrepreneurial plunge also. This book is just what women in the business world need today. Kudos for a job well done!

Cynthia Good
CEO & Editor, PINK Magazine

These all too familiar tales of the traps too many successful women find themselves in are told with an honesty that is refreshing. No path is easy, but knowing the one you are on isn't right for you is the first step in moving forward. The authors clearly explain how they learned to redefine success on their terms, thus finding the courage to do what they love.

Wendy Lopez
2009-10 Chair
National Association of Women Business Owners • www.nawbo.org

These four women are wonderful role models for people wanting to achieve a successful business and a balanced life. Their stories are a powerful testimonial to what it truly means to have a passion and commitment toward a worthy goal. Readers will use the authors' experiences as inspiration that will help them realize their own dreams.

(Continued next page)

Charles Oglesby
President & Chief Executive Officer
Asbury Automotive Group (NYSE ticker: ABG)
www.asburyautomotive.com

I started in business as a salesperson at car dealerships and, as such, I had to know my market, set my goals, motivate myself, and plan, execute, and follow up to meet my personal sales goals. But I never did have to wear every hat in the business. Therefore, let me tip my hat to these four women who successfully opened their own businesses and wear many hats. Their stories illustrate the challenges they faced as well as the many rewards of seeking their passions. We know small business is the backbone of the American economy. Marla, Peggy, Eleanor, and Angela show us why that backbone is so strong. Enjoy!

Pamela Chambers O'Rourke
President & CEO
ICON Information Consultants, LP • www.iconconsultants.com

The authors of this book have really captured the essence of following your instinct and conscience when deciding a path in life and career. The book embodies the passion of life/work balance leading to ultimate happiness and calm contentment in one's life. I followed a similar path that led me to starting my own multi-million-dollar business. This book puts in perspective that you can be all you want to be — a mom, a role model, and an entrepreneur — by just listening to your gut and believing in your passions. As women we can achieve our utopia by just throwing one more ball into life's juggling act!

Deborah Britt Roebuck, Ph.D.
Professor of Management, Kennesaw State University, Coles College of Business
Kennesaw, Georgia • www.kennesaw.edu

Delightful, refreshing, and inspiring are words that flash through my mind as I think about the stories and the words of wisdom I read from each of these four uniquely different women. Their powerful stories resonated with me on so many levels. I was drawn immediately into their lives and could relate to their struggles, challenges, and journeys as they evolved into the wonderful female leaders they are today.

Being a lifelong learner myself, I loved the role reading and learning played and, in all likelihood, continues to play in their lives. Their stories brought forth memories of when I went to elementary school and how I stopped at the library every day after school.

When Marla and Peggy spoke about feelings of living two lives and not having self-confidence, I sensed their pain and once again could empathize. While I pursued my Ph.D., I struggled, too, with whether I was sacrificing my family for my work. At the time it seemed the best choice; but even today I sometimes wonder if I made the right decision. So reading how others have faced similar challenges has made me to realize I am not alone in my thoughts regarding choices I have made.

Like Marla, I am largely a generalist, and it has helped in my career to play different roles and to take on new responsibilities. However, like Peggy, I do think you need a niche and that you should play to your strengths.

Like Peggy, I have lacked self-confidence and had to learn to believe in myself. Nevertheless, as Eleanor shared, I gained that self-confidence through building relationships with others who would provide the support and coaching I needed.

When Angela stated that we should never underestimate the power of language used well and the pleasing placement of that language on a piece of paper, I immediately knew this was one woman who truly understood the power of words and knew that we don't get a second chance in this frantic, hectic world. First impressions, as Angela stated, make an impact that is difficult to change.

When I read how Angela and Peggy either worked free or for little compensation, I thought, "me, too" and wondered why we sell ourselves short. Thus, my hope for the younger generation is that they will learn and not repeat our mistakes.

I, like these authors, believe our faith helps sustain us through trials and tribulations. My faith has helped me face exciting new adventures that I never thought this little farmer's daughter from Missouri would experience. However, as Angela, Eleanor, Marla, and Peggy have so eloquently stated, we sometimes have to get out of our own way by recognizing our fears and our own self-imposed assumptions and beliefs. Alternatively, we will not grow both personally and professionally.

My husband and I have run a small family business in addition to our full-time jobs. Much as Eleanor and her husband have faced, Rob and I have faced the realization that our children may not want to take over the business. Sometimes, as Eleanor shared, you think you are making life better for your children, only to have them want to pursue their own dreams. Nevertheless, as Eleanor stated, it is your dream, not their dream. Therefore, like the Mother Eagle, you have to push your children out of the nest so they will fly and soar in the direction they choose.

All of these women's stories overflowed with examples of the importance of helping and supporting others, embracing opportunities to learn, and believing in one's self. These are valuable lessons for all women to learn. The words of advice that follow the stories are priceless. I encourage young entrepreneurs to take advantage of the guidance that these authors and business leaders so willingly share. Take some time to read this book and I truly believe you will see it as a good investment of your time.

NOTES: